ATLAS

2

Learning-Centered Communication

David Nunan

Heinle & Heinle Publishers
A Division of Wadsworth, Inc.
Boston, MA 02116, U.S.A.

The publication of ATLAS was directed by the members of the Heinle & Heinle Global Innovations Publishing Team:

Elizabeth Holthaus, ESL Team Leader
David C. Lee, Editorial Director
John F. McHugh, Market Development Director
Lisa McLaughlin, Production Editor
Nancy Mann, Developmental Editor

Also participating in the publication of the program were:

Publisher: Stanley J. Galek
Assistant Editor: Kenneth Mattsson
Manufacturing Coordinator: Mary Beth Hennebury
Full-Service Design and Production: Ligature, Inc.

Manufactured in the United States of America.

ISBN: 0-08384-4086-X

Heinle & Heinle Publishers is a division of Wadsworth, Inc.

10 9 8 7 6

Preface

Atlas is a four-level ESL/EFL course for young adults and adults. Its learner-centered, task-based approach motivates learners and helps to create an active, communicative classroom.

Atlas develops the four language skills of listening, speaking, reading, and writing in a systematic and integrated fashion. Each level is designed to cover from 60 to 90 hours of classroom instruction. It can also be adapted for shorter or longer courses; suggestions for doing so are provided in the teacher's extended edition.

Each level of Atlas consists of the following components:

Student's Book: The student's book contains 12 "core" units and 3 review units. Following the 15 units are "Communication Challenges," which provide extra communicative practice to conclude each unit. Grammar summaries for each unit appear at the end of the book, along with an irregular verb chart.

Teacher's Extended Edition: The teacher's extended edition contains an introduction to the philosophy of the course, general guidelines for teaching with Atlas, detailed teaching suggestions for each unit, and extension activities. It also includes the tapescript and answer keys for the textbook and the workbook.

Teacher Tape: The tape contains spoken material for all of the listening activities in the student text.

Workbook: The workbook provides practice and expansion of the vocabulary, structures, functions, and learning strategies in the student text.

Workbook Tape: The workbook tape contains spoken material for all of the listening activities in the workbook.

Video: The video, which contains lively, real-life material, provides reinforcement and expansion of the topics and functions found in the student text.

Assessment Package: The assessment package will be available in 1995.

FEATURES	BENEFITS
Unit goals are explicitly stated at the beginning of each unit.	Awareness of goals helps students to focus their learning.
Listening and reading texts are derived from **high-interest, authentic source material.**	Naturalistic/realistic language prepares students for the language they will encounter outside the classroom.
Each unit is built around two **task chains**, sequences of tasks that are linked together in principled ways and in which succeeding tasks are built on those that come before.	Task chains enhance student interest and motivation by providing students with integrated learning experiences.
Units feature explicit focus on **learning strategies.**	Conscious development of a range of learning strategies helps students become more effective learners both in and out of class.
End-of-unit **Self-Check** section encourages students to record and reflect on what they have learned.	Developing personal records of achievement increases student confidence and motivation.

Table of Contents

Language Focus Structures	Learning Strategies	Communication Challenges
• statements and yes/no questions with *to be* • *wh* questions: *what* and *where* + *to be* • subject pronouns • possessive adjectives	• classifying* • selective listening • making inferences • scanning • personalizing • practicing	• information gap: listening
• statements and yes/no questions with *do/does* • *wh* questions with *do/does*	• predicting* • scanning • selective listening • personalizing • practicing	• describing families
• present-tense questions with *do/does:* a review • *wh* questions: *who* + *do/does*	• selective listening • personalizing • brainstorming* • scanning • practicing	• information gap: reading postcards
• simple present with *like* • adjectives	• classifying • personalizing • brainstorming • selective listening* • scanning • practicing	• information gap: matching descriptions and photographs
• modal: *can* • *How much? How many?*	• personalizing* • scanning • selective listening • brainstorming	• information gap: listening, reading, and writing—finding the best place for Teresa to live
• prepositions: *on, next to, near* • present progressive for actions in progress	• classifying • cooperating • scanning* • selective listening	• information gap: finding where services are located
• making suggestions with *Why don't you . . . ?* • *there is / there are* and *one, any, some*	• memorizing conversational patterns* • classifying • selective listening • practicing • scanning • cooperating • personalizing	• listening and speaking: touring and tracing the route

*The asterisked learning strategies are explicitly taught in the unit. The others are used passively.

Language Focus Structures	Learning Strategies	Communication Challenges
• adverbs of frequency • modal: *should*	• scanning • cooperating* • selective listening • personalizing • making inferences • practicing	• information gap: reading about foreign cities
• simple past: statements and yes/no questions • simple past: connecting words and *wh* questions	• brainstorming • personalizing • selective listening • discovering* • practicing • cooperating	• information gap: talking about popular weekend activities
• present progressive for planned future • intensifiers: *too, fairly, pretty, very*	• brainstorming • personalizing • selective listening • practicing* • discovering	• making suggestions about entertainment and leisure activities
• present perfect and *Have you ever . . . ?* • time expressions and *How often . . . ?*	• personalizing • classifying • selective listening • making inferences • scanning • role-playing*	• role-playing: scenes at a health club
• comparisons with adjectives • modals: *have to, should, could*	• brainstorming • selective listening • scanning • cooperating • skimming* • practicing	• information gap: talking about jobs

*The asterisked learning strategies are explicitly taught in the unit. The others are used passively.

Acknowledgments

Many people were involved in the planning and development of Atlas, and it is impossible for me to mention them all by name. However, special thanks must go to the following:

The reviewers, who helped to shape Atlas:

Lucia de Aragão, Uniao Cultural, São Paulo, **Eric Beatty**, Institut Franco-Américain, Rennes, **Rosamunde Blanck**, City University of New York, Hiroshima, **Richard Berwick**, University of British Columbia, Vancouver, **Jennifer Bixby**, Acton, Massachusetts, **Eric Bray**, YMCA English School, Kyoto, **Vincent Broderick**, Soai College, Osaka, **Chiou-Lan Chern**, Tunghai University, Taichung, **Katy Cox**, Casa Thomas Jefferson, Brasilia, **Richard Evanoff**, Aoyama Gakuin University, Tokyo, **Charles Frederickson, Katherine Harrington**, Associacao Alumni, São Paulo, **Phyllis Herrin de Obregon**, Universidade Autonoma de Querétaro, Querétaro, **James Kahny**, Language Institute of Japan, Tokyo, **Thomas Kanemoto**, Kanda Institute of Foreign Languages, Tokyo, **Maidy Kiji**, Konan Women's University, Kobe, **Richard Klecan**, Miyagi Gakuin, Sendai, **Susan Kobashigawa, Thomas Kral**, United States Information Agency, Washington, D.C., **David Levy**, McGill University, Montreal, **Angela Llanas**, Instituto Anglo-Mexicano, Mexico City, **Thomas Long**, ELS International, Seoul, **David Ludwig**, Crane Publishing Company, Taipei, **Carole McCarthy**, CEGEP ST-Hyacinthe, Quebec, **Jane McElroy**, University of Rio Grande, Tokyo, **John Moore and Aviva Smith**, ECC Foreign Language Institute, Tokyo, **Rebecca Oxford**, University of Alabama, Tuscaloosa, **Margene Petersen**, ELS, Philadelphia, Pennsylvania, **James Riordan and Adelaide Oliveira**, Associacao Cultural, Salvador, **Andrea Safire**, Berkeley, California, **Charles Sandy**, Chubu University Junior College, Nagoya, **Tamara Swenson**, Osaka Jogakuin Junior College, Osaka

The teachers and students in the following institutions, who field-tested early versions of Atlas and provided invaluable comments and suggestions:

AEON, Japan, **Aoyama Gakuin University**, Tokyo, **Associacao Alumni**, São Paulo, **Associacao Cultural**, Salvador, **Associacao Cultural**, Ribeirão Prêto, **AEON**, **Boston University**, Boston, Massachusetts, **Centro Cultural Brasil–Estados Unidos**, Campinas, **Concordia University**, Montreal, **ELS International**, Seoul, **GEOS**, Japan, **Huron University**, Tokyo, **Instituto Anglo-Mexicano**, Mexico City, **Konan Women's University**, Kobe, **LaGuardia Community College**, Long Island City, New York, **Miyagi Gakuin**, Sendai, **Osaka Jogakuin Junior College**, Osaka, **SHOWA Women's University**, Boston, Massachusetts, **Soai College**, Osaka, **Southwest Community College**, Los Angeles, **Tokyo Foreign Language College**, Tokyo, **Universidade Autonoma de Querétaro**, Querétaro, **Waseda University**, Tokyo, **YMCA English School**, Kyoto

Other reviewers, too numerous to mention, helped make this course what it is. Particular thanks must go to Ellen Shaw, who is quite simply the best editor in the business and whose detailed editing and comments strengthened the materials in many different ways. Thanks also to Clarice Lamb, whose unflinching faith in the project helped me maintain my own faith through periods of difficulty and doubt.

I should also like to acknowledge and thank the various International Thomson Publishing and Heinle & Heinle representatives who facilitated field testing and whose personal assistance during visits associated with the development and promotion of Atlas was invaluable. I should like to thank Robert Cullen in Singapore, Carol Chen in Taipei, and Hisae Inami in Tokyo for their particular assistance and support.

Particular thanks are due to my editors at Heinle & Heinle, who helped at all stages in the planning and development of Atlas. Special thanks are due to Charlie Heinle and Stan Galek, for their personal interest and support from the very beginning of the project; to José Wehnes, for his unique marketing philosophy; to Dave Lee, who helped guide the project; to Chris Foley, who helped shape the initial philosophy; to Meg Morris, for her research and data-gathering skills; and to Lisa McLaughlin, for her dedication to ensuring the visual appeal of the book. Most of all, thanks are due to my developmental editor, Nancy Mann, for her professional skills, her quiet good humor, and her happy acceptance of late-night calls.

1 New People

Warm-Up

Unit Goals

In this unit you will:

Exchange personal information

"My name is Mike. What's your name?"

"Where are you from?"

"I'm from Tokyo."

Describe yourself and other people

"I'm twenty-three. I have dark hair."

"Laura is fifty-five. She has green eyes."

Introduce others

"This is Yoko."

---

1 Look at the picture. Where are these people? At school? At a party? At work? How do you know?

2 a Pair Work Check [√] the words you both know.

- ☐ big
- ☐ twenty
- ☐ elderly
- ☐ eighteen
- ☐ dark hair
- ☐ a white beard
- ☐ short
- ☐ young
- ☐ twenty-three
- ☐ old
- ☐ tall
- ☐ a beard
- ☐ dark eyes
- ☐ middle-aged
- ☐ blond hair
- ☐ teenage
- ☐ small
- ☐ blue eyes

b Find words that describe the people in the picture. Write them down.

....

3 Group Work Listen. Then practice the conversation.

A: Hello. My name's Mike.
B: Pleased to meet you, Mike. I'm Yoko. This is Noriko.
C: Nice to meet you, Mike.
A: Nice to meet you, Noriko.

Work with another student. Introduce yourselves. Now introduce your partner to some other students.

Task Chain 1 Giving personal information

Conversation ....

Conversation ....

Conversation ....

Task 1

a Look at the people in the pictures. Where are they? In a train station? At an airport? How do you know?

b 🎧 Listen to conversations 1, 2, and 3. Write the number of each conversation under the picture that illustrates it.

c What happened to Mike's bag?

Task 2

a Check [√] the words or phrases you know. Compare your checklist with another student's list.

☐ Last name   ☐ Telephone number
☐ First name   ☐ Date of birth
☐ Address   ☐ Occupation

b 🎧 Mike is talking to a police officer. Listen to the conversation. Look at the list above and circle the words you hear.

Task 3

🎧 Listen to the conversation again and then fill out the form below.

California State Police

San Francisco International Airport
Mon.–Fri. 10 a.m.–1 p.m. 2 p.m.–5 p.m.

Incident #: _____

Date: _____

Incident Report

Name: _____

Address: _____
(Street)   (City)   (State)

Telephone: _____

Date of Birth: _____

Occupation: _____

Problem: black travel bag missing

_____

where
ou're invited... go to the movies! meet me for lunch
what do you do?
why
s my family when neighborhood

Dear Mike,

Hello from San Francisco. I told your brother that I can pick you up at the airport on Sunday. Let's meet at your boarding gate. I'm twenty years old, I'm short and I have red hair and green eyes. Your brother says you are tall and have dark hair and blue eyes. I guess we won't have any trouble finding each other.

Sincerely,

Marcia de Beridino

Mr. M. Frota
1600 26th Street
Chicago, IL 60606

USA 29

Task 4

Someone Mike does not know is meeting him at the airport. Read this postcard and circle the words that describe people.

Put the color, age, and size words from the postcard in the correct columns.

COLOR	AGE	SIZE

Task 5

"I'm twenty-one. I'm short and heavy. I have dark curly hair, blue eyes, and very big ears. My friends call me Shorty, but you can call me Dave."

Pair Work Now write some sentences about yourself. Exchange papers with your partner.

Task 6

Group Work Discussion. Different cultures describe people in different ways. In North America, people use size, weight, eye and hair color, age. How do you describe people in your culture?

Language Focus 1 Statements and yes/no questions with *to be*

1 🎧 **Pair Work** Listen. Then practice this conversation.

A: So I'll meet you at Gate 11 at 9:30. Now, what do you look like?

B: Well, I'm twenty-one. I'm of average height and weight. I have dark curly hair and brown eyes.

A: OK.

B: And I'm with my girlfriend. She's nineteen. She's tall, and she has blond hair and blue eyes. You can't miss us!

2 **Pair Work** Which words do you move to make questions? Draw arrows to show your answers.

a You (are) Tomoko.

b I am late.

c His girlfriend is nineteen.

d Mike is from Chicago.

e It is early.

f You are students.

g Your name is Mike.

h They are from Korea.

3 Match these questions and answers and then practice with another student.

Questions
a Are you Alex?
b Is Sandra your girlfriend?
c Am I right?
d Is your girlfriend nineteen?
e Are they students?

Answers
.... Yes, you are.
.... Yes, she is.
.... Yes, they are.
.... Yes, she is.
.... Yes, I am.

4 **Pair Work** Someone is meeting you at the airport. Describe yourself. Use the conversation in activity 1 as an example.

Do you know the rule?

To turn statements with *to be* into yes/no questions, move *am, is, are* to ....

?

Task Chain 2 Making new friends

Task 1

🎧 Mike arrives at a party for new students. Listen to the conversation. How many people does he meet? Circle your answer.

1   2   3   4   5

Task 2

🎧 Listen again and complete the statements.

a Mike introduces himself. He says: " _Hello, I'm Mike_ ."
b John introduces Anna. He says: " ."
c Mike greets Anna. He says: " ."
d John introduces Maggie. He says: " ."

Task 3

Here are some ways to introduce yourself and other people. Write the letters in the correct columns in the chart.

a I'm Pete Carlton.
b I'd like you to meet Paula.
c My name's Nina.
d This is Carmel.
e I want you to meet Ms. Shaw.

INTRODUCING YOURSELF	INTRODUCING SOMEONE ELSE

Task 4

You choose: Do Ⓐ or Ⓑ.

Ⓐ **Pair Work** Discussion. How do you introduce yourself in your own language? How do you introduce someone else?

Ⓑ **Pair Work** Discussion. How do you feel when you meet new people? Embarrassed? Shy? Frightened? Interested? Bored? Excited? Talk about how you feel.

A I'm very shy. I'm embarrassed when I meet new people.

B Oh, really? Not me! I'm interested in new people.

Task 5

a **Group Work** Discussion. This chart shows where single people meet each other in the United States. What do you think the percentages are in your country?

How do single men and women meet each other?

	% of men	% of women
Through friends	30%	36%
At parties	22%	18%
At bars, discos	24%	18%
At singles parties/dances	14%	18%
At work	10%	9%
Through newspaper ads	1%	1%
Don't remember	1%	2%

Adapted from: Margaret K. Ambry, *The Almanac of Consumer Markets*, Probus Publishing Co. Chicago, Ill.,1989.

b **Group Work** Discussion. Where can you meet new people?

	Yes	No
At school?	☐	☐
At a party?	☐	☐
At the movies?	☐	☐
At a shopping center?	☐	☐
At a sports event?	☐	☐
At a concert?	☐	☐
At a friend's home?	☐	☐
....	☐	☐
....	☐	☐
....	☐	☐
....	☐	☐

Add to the list and ask some other students.

Language Focus 2 *Wh* questions: *what* and *where* + *to be*

1 a 🎧 **Pair Work** Listen. Then practice the conversation.

> **A:** Hi! I'm Yongsue. What's your name?
> **B:** Vera.
> **A:** Where are you from?
> **B:** Chicago. What about you?
> **A:** I'm from Seoul, Korea. What do you do?
> **B:** I'm a student. What do you do?
> **A:** I'm a student, too.

b **Pair Work** Now use information that is true for you.

2 Fill in the blanks.

Questions	Answers
a What's .... name?	My .... Mike.
b Where .... you from?	Mike .... from Chicago.
c Where .... he from?	He .... from France.
d What .... name?	Her .... Yumi.
e Where .... she from?	.... from Japan.
f What .... his name?	His .... Michael.
g What .... their names?	.... names are Miguel and Mercedes.
h Where .... they from?	They .... from Spain.

3 **Pair Work** Ask and answer these questions.

Questions	Answers
a What is Mike's last name?	*His last name is Frota.*
b Where is Mike from?	
c Where are Miguel and Mercedes from?	
d Where is Yumi from?	

4 **Pair Work** Ask and answer these questions.

Questions	Answers
a What's .... ?	My name ....
b Where .... from?	I'm ....
c What .... do?	I ....

Now describe your partner to another pair.

Example: "This is Angela. She's from Mexico City, and she's a nurse."

Self-Check

COMMUNICATION CHALLENGE

Look at Challenge 1 on page 111.

1 Write down five new words you learned in this unit.

....

2 Write down three new sentences or questions you learned.

....

....

....

3 Review the language skills you practiced in this unit.
Check [√] your answers.

CAN YOU:

Exchange personal information? ☐ yes ☐ a little ☐ not yet
Find or give an example: ....

Describe yourself and others? ☐ yes ☐ a little ☐ not yet
Find or give an example: ....

Introduce people? ☐ yes ☐ a little ☐ not yet
Find or give an example: ....

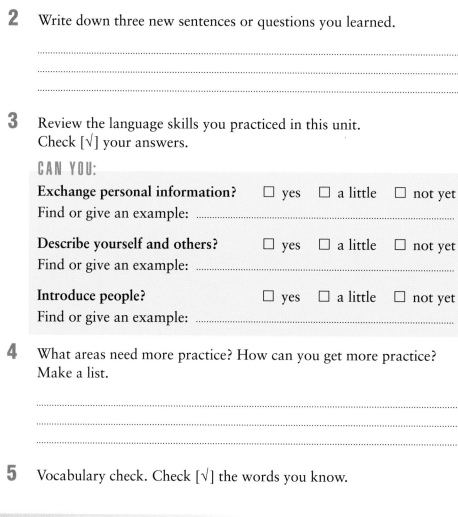

"I do workbook exercises to practice filling in personal information on forms."

"I practice describing myself in front of a mirror."

"I practice introductions with a partner after class."

4 What areas need more practice? How can you get more practice? Make a list.

....

....

....

5 Vocabulary check. Check [√] the words you know.

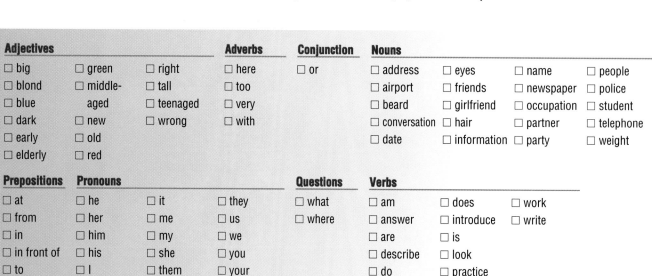

Adjectives			Adverbs	Conjunction	Nouns			
☐ big	☐ green	☐ right	☐ here	☐ or	☐ address	☐ eyes	☐ name	☐ people
☐ blond	☐ middle-	☐ tall	☐ too		☐ airport	☐ friends	☐ newspaper	☐ police
☐ blue	aged	☐ teenaged	☐ very		☐ beard	☐ girlfriend	☐ occupation	☐ student
☐ dark	☐ new	☐ wrong	☐ with		☐ conversation	☐ hair	☐ partner	☐ telephone
☐ early	☐ old				☐ date	☐ information	☐ party	☐ weight
☐ elderly	☐ red							

Prepositions	Pronouns			Questions	Verbs		
☐ at	☐ he	☐ it	☐ they	☐ what	☐ am	☐ does	☐ work
☐ from	☐ her	☐ me	☐ us	☐ where	☐ answer	☐ introduce	☐ write
☐ in	☐ him	☐ my	☐ we		☐ are	☐ is	
☐ in front of	☐ his	☐ she	☐ you		☐ describe	☐ look	
☐ to	☐ I	☐ them	☐ your		☐ do	☐ practice	

2 Meet the Family

Warm-Up

Unit Goals

In this unit you will:

Talk about your family

"I have a brother and two sisters."

Ask about other people's families

"How many sisters do you have?"

LEARNING STRATEGY

Predicting = saying what you think will happen.

1 Look at the title and the goals of this unit. They can help you predict what the unit is about. What do you think you will do in this unit?

This is what one student predicted:
"I'll listen to people talk about their families."
"I'll describe my family."

Pair Work Can you predict some of the things you will do in this unit? Now look quickly through the unit. Were you right?

Picture 1  Picture 2

Picture 3  Picture 4

Picture 5  Picture 6

2 Match these descriptions with the families in the pictures above.

Descriptions	*Picture*
a A family with one parent, one stepparent, and children	6
b A family with two parents and one adopted child	....
c A family with two parents and two children	....
d A family with two parents and three children	....
e A single-parent family	....
f A family with one grandparent, two parents, and children	....

3 a Which family photograph shows a "typical" North American family?

b What is a typical family in your country? Is the typical family changing?

Task Chain 1 Meeting the family

Task 1

Are these family members male or female? Write *M* for male or *F* for female.

M. uncle	.... father	.... aunt
F. grandmother	.... daughter	.... brother
.... son	.... grandfather	.... mother
.... niece	.... sister	.... stepfather
.... nephew	.... brother-in-law	

Task 2

a 🎧 Vera is talking about the people in the photograph. Listen and check [√] the words you hear.

☐ grandfather   ☐ brother
☐ dad   ☐ daughter
☐ mom   ☐ niece
☐ sister   ☐ uncle
☐ son   ☐ nephew

b 🎧 Listen again and check [√] the names you hear.

☐ Maria   ☐ Cristina
☐ Vera   ☐ Bobbie
☐ Juan   ☐ Sandra
☐ José   ☐ Jean

Task 3

🎧 **Pair Work** Listen again and find these people: Vera, Vera's grandfather, Vera's mom, José, Juan, Cristina, Sandra. Label the people in the photo.

Task 4

Complete this family tree for Vera's family.

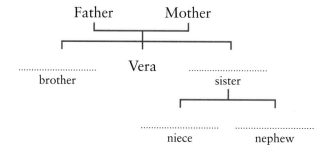

Task 5

Now draw your own family tree.

A Do you have any sisters?

B Yes, I do. I have two sisters, Maggie and Janice.

Task 6

a Pair Work Ask questions about your partner's family. Now draw your partner's family tree.

b Pair Work Exchange roles and do the task again.

Task 7

Group Work Survey. Talk to four other students and complete the survey chart.

STUDENT'S NAME	BROTHER'S OR SISTER'S NAME	LIVE WITH PARENTS	WORK OR SCHOOL	JOB OR FIELD OF STUDY
Somchai	Suphat	no	work	doctor

a Do you have a brother or a sister?
b Does he or she live with your parents?
c Does he or she work or go to school?
d What is his or her job or field of study?

Pair Work Now work with a student from another group. Report on your survey.

Example: "Kenji has a sister. Her name is Tomoko. She lives in Kobe. She's a teller. She works in a bank."

Language Focus 1 Statements and yes/no questions with *do/does*

1 **Pair Work** Fill in the blanks. Then practice the questions and answers.

Questions   *Answers*

.... I have time to call? Yes, you .... No, ... don't.

.... you have a brother? Yes, I .... No, I ....

.... she have an aunt? Yes, ... does. No, she ....

.... he have an uncle? Yes, he .... No, he ....

.... you have a sister? Yes, ... do. No, we ....

.... they have children? Yes, they .... No, they ....

2 **a** 🎧 **Pair Work** Listen. Then practice this conversation.

A: Do you have any brothers or sisters, Helen?

B: Yes, I do. I have two brothers and three sisters. I also have six aunts and eight uncles and 25 cousins.

A: Do you have nieces and nephews?

B: Yes, I do—my sister's kids. They live with us.

b **Pair Work** Now use information that is true for you.

3 **Pair Work** Ask and answer these questions.

Example: "Does Helen have three sisters?" "Yes, she does."

a Does Helen have five aunts?

b Does she have a sister?

c Does she have a brother?

d Does she have six uncles?

e Does she have any cousins?

f Does she have nieces?

g Do they live with her?

Do you know the rule?

Fill in the blanks with the correct pronouns from this list: *I, you, he, she, it, we, they.*

Use *do* with ....

Use *does* with ....

4 **Group Work** Class survey. Ask your classmates questions like this: "Do you go to the movies often?" Write one name in each box in the chart. See how many boxes you can fill.

FIND SOMEONE WHO . . .	YES	NO
likes hamburgers		
plays tennis		
speaks three languages		
likes classical music		
goes to the movies often		
wants to be an actor		
lives alone		
likes modern art		
drives a car		
works at night		

Task Chain 2 Talking about your family

Task 1

These people are on a television game show. They are talking about themselves and their families.

a Can you predict some of words you will hear? Write them in the chart at left.

b 🎧 Listen. Check [√] the words you hear in the chart at left.

PREDICT	LISTEN
sisters	√

Task 2

🎧 Listen again and fill in this chart.

NAME	AGE	OCCUPATION	FAMILY
Eva	21	?	3 sisters, 4 brothers

Task 3

a 🎧 In the next quiz show, the contestants are playing a game called *Know Your In-Laws*. Listen to the first part of the conversation and find out how the game is played.

b 🎧 Listen again and write the questions in the chart.

c 🎧 Listen once more and write the answers in the chart.

QUESTIONS	JAMES'S ANSWERS	MARY'S ANSWERS

A What does Tomoko's father do?

B He's a lawyer.

A Where is his office?

B I don't know.

Task 4

a **Pair Work** You have five minutes to find out as much as you can about your partner's family.

b **Group Work** Now work with another pair. Ask questions about the other partners' families.

c **Group Work** Discussion. Who collected the most information?

Language Focus 2 *Wh* questions with *do/does*

1 🎧 Pair Work Listen. Then practice this conversation.

A: Who's that?
B: That's my brother.
A: Great-looking guy. What's his name?
B: Joe.
A: And what does he do?
B: He goes to school.
A: Oh, where does he go?
B: He goes to McGill University in Montreal.

2 Pair Work Fill in the blanks and practice the questions and answers.

Questions	*Answers*
a What .... I need?	You .... a work permit.
b What do .... do?	I .... a teacher.
c Where .... he work?	.... works in a bank.
d Where .... you go to school?	We .... to Boston University.
e What .... they do?	They .... students.

3 Pair Work Write questions for these answers. Then practice them.

Questions	*Answers*
a ....?	I live in Mexico.
b ....?	She's a nurse.
c ....?	They go to Hunter College.
d ....?	We come from Tokyo.
e ....?	They're students.

4 a Turn these statements into questions with *do/does*.

I need a work permit.
I need ... *what* ....
... *what* .... I need
... *What do I* .... need?

He studies engineering.
he studies ....
.... he studies
.... study?

She lives in Tokyo.
she lives ....
.... she lives
.... live?

You go to City University.
you go ....
.... you go
.... go?

b What is the pattern for these kinds of questions? Number the following words to put them in order.

.... **noun/pronoun**   .... **verb**   .... *wh* **word**   .... **do/does**

Self-Check

COMMUNICATION CHALLENGE

Look at Challenge 2 on page 112.

1 Write down five new words you learned in this unit.

....

2 Write down three new sentences or questions you learned.

....

....

....

3 Review the language skills you practiced in this unit. Check [√] your answers.

CAN YOU:

Talk about your family? ☐ yes ☐ a little ☐ not yet
Find or give an example: ....

Ask about other people's families? ☐ yes ☐ a little ☐ not yet
Find or give an example: ....

"I listen to the cassette tape at home and repeat the conversations."

"Tomoko and I practice the conversations outside of class."

"I talk about my friends' families during coffee break."

4 What areas need more practice? How can you get more practice? Make a list.

....

....

....

....

5 Vocabulary check. Check [√] the words you know.

Adjective	Conjunction	Nouns				Verbs		Prepositions
☐ typical	☐ and	☐ aunt	☐ family	☐ male	☐ school	☐ ask	☐ have	☐ about
		☐ brother	☐ father	☐ mom	☐ sister	☐ come	☐ live	☐ for
		☐ child	☐ female	☐ mother	☐ son	☐ draw	☐ need	
		☐ children	☐ grandfather	☐ nephew	☐ television	☐ find	☐ predict	
		☐ dad	☐ grandmother	☐ niece	☐ uncle	☐ give	☐ study	
		☐ daughter	☐ home	☐ parent	☐ work	☐ go	☐ talk	
		☐ dictionary	☐ kids	☐ photograph		☐ has	☐ tell	

3 Old Friends

Unit Goals

In this unit you will:

Talk about friends
"Tomoko is kind."

Ask for information about other people
"Who is that?"
"Who do you work with?"

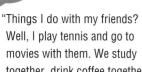

"Things I do with my friends? Well, I play tennis and go to movies with them. We study together, drink coffee together, and talk on the phone."

Warm-Up

1 The photographs above show groups of friends. Which groups look interesting? Why?

2 Listen. Maria is talking about two of the pictures. Which ones is she talking about?

3 **Pair Work** Think of your best friends. What do you do together?

- ☐ play tennis
- ☐ go to movies
- ☐ go to parties
- ☐ have coffee
- ☐ talk on the phone

Add your own.

....
....
....

Task Chain 1 Close friends

"Charlie is smart and good-looking, Tomoko is serious and intelligent, and Somchai is funny and outgoing."

Task 1

a Pair Work Which words would you use to describe your best friend? Circle them. What qualities are most important in a friend?

happy	serious	smart	good-looking
romantic	funny	sexy	intelligent
outgoing	interesting	kind	

b Pair Work Can you add any other words to the list?

c Pair Work Think of three friends and make statements about them. Use words from the list above.

Task 2

 Listen to the conversation. Tony is talking about his best friends. Check [√] the names you hear and write occupations next to them.

Occupations

☐ Dave ....

☐ Victor ....

☐ Tina ....

☐ Tony ....

☐ Maria ....

☐ Pete ....

☐ Pamela ....

☐ Maggie ....

☐ Steve ....

Task 3

GroupWork Look at the photographs on page 25. Find a picture of Tony and his friends. Give a reason for your choice.

Task 4

GroupWork Discussion. What does Tony do? Is this an unusual occupation for a man? What about in your country? Do men do this job? What jobs do men rarely do? What jobs do women rarely do?

Task 5

a PairWork Read these messages and write the missing names in the blanks. Use the conversation in Task 2 and the messages to figure out the names.

"One of my best friends is Vanessa, who is a photographer. We met in college. We go swimming and dancing together, and we talk about work, money, and our other friends."

Task 6

a Think of three good friends, and then complete the chart.

b PairWork Now use the information to talk about your friends with a partner.

NAME	THINGS YOU DO TOGETHER	THINGS YOU TALK ABOUT	OCCUPATION	WHERE YOU MET
1				
2				
3				

Language Focus 1 Present-tense questions with *do/does:* a review

1 🎧 **Pair Work** Listen. Then practice the conversation.

A: Do you have a best friend?
B: Yes, Tomoko.
A: What does she do?
B: She's a student.
A: What do you do together?
B: Oh, we study together. Sometimes we go to the movies.

Most people form their closest relationships in high school, at college, or at work. In North America, many high school students have a boyfriend or a girlfriend. Many people start dating in their early teens, and they have a steady boyfriend or girlfriend by the time they are 16. The average North American has his or her first "puppy love" at age 13 and first serious love at age 17.

In some countries, it is unusual for young people to have a steady boyfriend or girlfriend until they finish high school. In fact, in some countries, young people are not allowed even to talk to members of the opposite sex. In these cultures, it is common to see young men going out with other young men and young women going out with other young women.

2 **Group Work** Discussion. Read the newspaper article at left and discuss the questions that follow.

In your country . . .
- do young people go on dates alone or in groups?
- when do people start dating?
- do men go out with each other in groups?
- do women go out with each other in groups?
- where do people usually go on dates?

3 **Pair Work** Fill in the blanks. Then practice the questions and answers.

	Questions	*Answers*	
a	.... I need a student card?	Yes, you	No, ... don't.
b	What does your sister do?	She	
c	.... she have a close friend?	Yes, ... does.	No, she ....
d	Where does .... work?	He	
e	.... we need a ticket?	Yes, you	No, ... don't.
f	Do .... have girlfriends?	Yes, they	No, ... don't.

4 **Pair Work** Ask and answer these questions.

	Questions	*Answers*
a	Do you like pop music?	....
b	Where does your best friend live?	....
c	Do you have a brother?	....
d	Does your mother speak English?	....
e	When do you get up in the morning?	....
f	Do you like sports?	....
g	What do you usually do after class?	....
h	Do you have a girlfriend/boyfriend/ wife/husband?	....
i	Does your best friend go to school?	....

Task 1

🎧 **Pair Work** Listen. Then practice the conversation.

A: Hi, Jenny. How is school?
B: Fine.
A: It must be lonely in a new city.
B: It is a little. But I have some new friends.
A: That's nice.
B: And I see my classmates every day.

Task 2

🎧 Listen. Victor is doing a survey. What does he want to know?

Task 3

🎧 Listen again. Check [√] the names you hear.

☐ Tony	☐ Sonia	☐ Uncle Carlos
☐ Victor	☐ Nina	☐ Ms. Mills
☐ Maria	☐ Agnes	☐ Ms. Miller
☐ Mary	☐ Annie	☐ Sam
☐ Steve	☐ Uncle Charles	☐ Mrs. Williams
☐ Sophie	☐ Karen	

Task 4

Pair Work Who does Tony talk to every day? Complete the social network below.

....
(Boss)

....   *Parents*
(Girlfriend)   ....

....   **TONY**   ....
(Coworkers)   (Friends)

....
(Landlady)   (Bus driver)

....
(Uncle)

A Who do you talk to every day, Julio?

B Well, I talk to my parents, the people at work, and my girlfriend. What about you?

A I talk to my landlady, the guy in the coffee shop, and my roommate.

LEARNING STRATEGY

Brainstorming = thinking of as many new words and ideas as you can.

Task 5

Group Work Who do you talk to every day? Make your own social network and share it with several classmates.

....

....

....   **YOU**   ....

....

....

Task 6

a **Group Work** What do you talk about with your close friends? Your classmates or coworkers? Teachers? Make lists.

What You Talk About With . . .

CLOSE FRIENDS	CLASSMATES OR COWORKERS	TEACHERS OR BOSSES

Here is what one group said that close friends talk about: *money, movies, what to do on the weekend, changing jobs, the environment, relationships, other people, vacations, learning English, growing old, accidents.*

b **Group Work** Compare your lists with another group's lists and note similarities and differences.

Language Focus 2 *Wh questions: who + do/does*

1 🎧 **Pair Work** Listen. Then practice the conversation.

A: Excuse me. I'm doing a survey for *People* magazine. Can I ask you some questions?
B: Sure.
A: First of all, what do you do?
B: I work in a bank. I'm a teller.
A: Uh-huh. And who do you spend most of your time with?
B: My friends and family.
A: Who is your best friend?
B: My husband, I guess.
A: OK. And who do you talk to every day?
B: Well, now, let's see. My husband, my children, the people I work with, and the bank customers.

2 Now practice the conversation using information that is true for you.

3 Make questions for these cues.

Cues	*Questions*
a I like someone.	*Who do you like* ?
b Someone likes me.	*Who likes you* ?
c Molly works with someone.	.... ?
d Peter lives with someone.	.... ?
e Someone studies with Tomoko.	.... ?
f They go out with someone.	.... ?
g Someone studies with me.	.... ?
h We play tennis with someone.	.... ?

4 **Pair Work** How many statements and questions can you make from these words?

every day	do	who	talk to
work with	he	does	they
every week	she	you	

5 **Pair Work** Look at the pictures at left. Who does Maria talk to each week? Take turns asking and answering the following questions. Choose your answers from this list:

parents   friends   neighbor   bus driver   storekeeper

Who does Maria talk to at home? At school? On the bus? At the deli? At the coffee shop? On the way to school?

Self-Check

COMMUNICATION CHALLENGE

Pair Work Student A: Look at Challenge 3A on page 113. Student B: Look at Challenge 3B on page 115.

"I have a Canadian friend. She tells me when I make mistakes."

"This week, I'm going to ask five *who* questions every day."

1 Write down five new words you learned in this unit.

....

2 Write down three new sentences or questions you learned.

....

....

....

3 Review the language skills you practiced in this unit. Check [√] your answers.

CAN YOU:

Talk about friends? ☐ yes ☐ a little ☐ not yet
Find or give an example: ....

Ask for information about other people? ☐ yes ☐ a little ☐ not yet
Find or give an example: ....

4 What areas need more practice? How can you get more practice? Make a list.

....

....

....

....

5 Vocabulary check. Check [√] the words you know.

Adjectives		Conjunction	Nouns		Preposition	Question	Verbs	
☐ best	☐ kind	☐ but	☐ actor	☐ nurse	☐ with	☐ who	☐ brainstorm	☐ drink
☐ close	☐ lonely		☐ bank	☐ quality			☐ change	☐ grow
☐ funny	☐ outgoing		☐ bank teller	☐ secretary			☐ compare	☐ like
☐ good-looking	☐ romantic		☐ bus driver	☐ singer			☐ date	☐ play
	☐ serious		☐ coworker	☐ sports			☐ discuss	
☐ happy	☐ sexy		☐ culture	☐ teacher				
☐ intelligent	☐ smart		☐ hospital	☐ tomorrow				
☐ interesting	☐ unusual		☐ movies	☐ vacations				

4 Interesting People

Warm-Up

Unit Goals

In this unit you will:

Talk about occupations
"My brother is an actor."

Talk about likes and dislikes
"I don't like classical music."

Picture 1

Picture 2

Picture 3

1 Do you know these words to describe things? Circle the words you do not know and discuss them with your teacher.

strange	good-looking	beautiful	cute	good	old
funny	interesting	unusual	kind	silly	sad
young	handsome	energetic	ugly	lonely	evil
boring	intelligent	exciting	stupid	happy	

2 Pair Work Classify the words above into three groups: positive words, negative words, and neutral words.

POSITIVE	NEGATIVE	NEUTRAL
good	boring	unusual

3 Find two words to describe each of the pictures above.

Picture 1: .... Picture 2: .... Picture 3: ....
....

4 Group Work Pick three words to describe yourself and the other students in the group. Share these words with the rest of the class.

Task Chain 1 I like it a lot

Task 1

a **Pair Work** Brainstorm. Look at one of the pictures on page 33 for a few minutes, and check [√] all the words it reminds you of.

☐ beautiful ☐ funny ☐ exciting
☐ good ☐ stupid ☐ colorful
☐ ugly ☐ boring ☐ strange
☐ interesting ☐ unusual ☐ lonely
☐ sad

b Add three words of your own.

....

c **Group Work** Exchange lists with another pair, and guess which picture they looked at.

Task 2

Listen and answer the questions.

a How many people are talking? ....
b Where are they? ....
c What are they talking about? ....

Task 3

Listen again and check [√] these expressions when you hear them.

☐ I don't like it much.
☐ Yes, I like that one too.
☐ Which one do you like?
☐ I like that one.
☐ I like it a lot.
☐ I like it because of the colors and the shapes.

Task 4

Pair Work Listen again. Look at the pictures on page 33. Which two pictures are they talking about?

Task 5

a **Pair Work** Read these descriptions of the pictures on page 33 and guess which ones they are.

Pictures   *Descriptions*

....   This painting is interesting because of the colors and shapes. In fact, it doesn't even look much like a woman, but that doesn't matter.

....   This picture shows a beautiful young dancer at a famous night club.

....   This picture is very interesting because it's not clear what the women are looking at.

A The third picture is interesting.

B Well, it's unusual. But I think it's silly. It doesn't look like a girl at all.

b **Pair Work** Talk about the pictures on page 33. Follow the model, but use your own ideas.

Task 6

Group Work Survey. Find people who like the pictures on page 33 and people who dislike the pictures. Ask and answer questions.

Example: "Do you like picture 1?"   "Yes, I do."
                                       "No, I don't."

Write the people's names in the chart below.

	LIKES	DISLIKES
Picture 1		
Picture 2		
Picture 3		

Language Focus 1 Simple present with *like*

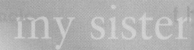

1 a 🎧 **Pair Work** Listen. Then practice the conversation.

> **A:** Do you like modern art?
> **B:** No, I don't like it very much. Do you like it?
> **A:** Yes, I do. What about music?
> **B:** I like rock music and jazz.
> **A:** So do I. I like classical music, too.
> **B:** What kind of movies do you like?
> **A:** I like thrillers.

b **Pair Work** Now give your own answers using words from these lists.

MUSIC	MOVIES
classical	comedies
jazz	thrillers
rock	westerns
country	romances

2 **Pair Work** Match these questions and answers. Then practice them.

Questions

a Do you like movies?
b What kind of art do you like?
c Does she like classical music?
d Does he like country music?
e Who is your favorite singer?
f Do they like modern dance?

Answers

.... No, she doesn't. She likes jazz.
.... I don't have one.
.... No, they don't. They like classical ballet.
.... Yes, I do. I like westerns.
.... I love modern art.
.... Yes, he does. He likes rock music, too.

3 **Pair Work** Fill in the blanks and practice the questions and answers.

Questions

a .... you like classical music?
b .... she like rock music?
c .... he like jazz?
d .... they like modern art?

Answers

Yes, I .... No, I ....
Yes, she .... No, she ....
Yes, he .... No, he ....
Yes, they .... No, they ....

4 **Pair Work** Use these cues to ask and answer questions.

Example: you / like / classical music
"Do you like classical music?" "Yes, I do." "No, I don't."

a what / movies / like
b you / like / horror movies
c what / favorite / music
d you / like / jazz

Task Chain 2 An unusual occupation

Task 1

a Do you know these occupations? Ask your teacher about the ones you don't know.

actor	lawyer	architect
musician	painter	doctor
receptionist	engineer	
writer	computer programmer	

b **Pair Work** Find an occupation that takes place . . .

in an office ....
in a TV studio ....
in a factory ....
at home ....
in a hospital ....

Task 2

Pair Work Check [√] the words that describe each occupation.

	INDOOR	OUTDOOR	HIGH-PAID	LOW-PAID	INTERESTING	BORING
actor						
architect						
computer programmer						
doctor						
engineer						
lawyer						
musician						
painter						
receptionist						
writer						

Task 3

🎧 Listen. Check [√] what kind of a program it is.

☐ a news broadcast   ☐ an interview   ☐ an advertisement

Task 4

🎧 Listen again. Check [√] the phrases you hear.

☐ a boring person   ☐ an interesting occupation
☐ an interesting person   ☐ a young man
☐ an unusual occupation   ☐ a strong man

Task 5

Are these statements true or false? Check [√] the correct answer.

		True	*False*
a	The interviewer is talking to Elvis Presley.	☐	☐
b	The person pretends to be Elvis Presley.	☐	☐
c	He earns $60,000 a year.	☐	☐
d	He plays the young Elvis.	☐	☐
e	Gary was a university professor.	☐	☐

Task 6

a Read this letter to a newspaper and complete the chart.

Dear Sir,
In Tuesday's newspaper, there was an article titled "Madonna, the $60 Million Woman." Everyone knows that she is a very rich woman. On the same page is an article about the salaries of college professors, who earn much less. Is it true that Madonna is much more important to society than a college professor? She entertains people, and they buy her CDs, play them a few times, and then forget them. What do professors do? They produce cures for cancer, they add to our knowledge, they train people to work for society. It seems that the more people earn, the less they help society.

(Professor) J. Stephen Smith

How Do They Help Society?

MADONNA	COLLEGE PROFESSORS
	produce cures for diseases

b **GroupWork** Discuss these questions. Give reasons for your answers.

- Do you think pop stars earn too much?
- Is it true that the more money people earn, the less they help society?
- What occupations are the most valuable to society?
- What occupations are the least valuable to society?

Language Focus 2 Adjectives

1 🎧 **Pair Work** Listen. Then practice the conversation.

A: Sandy, would you like to go on a date with my brother?
B: What's he like? Is he interesting?
A: Oh, yeah. He's an artist.
B: Is he good-looking?
A: Yes—very.
B: And is he nice?
A: Of course.
B: He sounds too good to be true!

2 **Group Work** Combine the following sentences.

a Madonna is rich. Madonna is a young woman.
  Madonna is a rich young woman.

b Paul is talented. Paul is a young actor.

....

c The *Mona Lisa* is famous. The *Mona Lisa* is an old painting.

....

d Eri is hard-working. Eri is a young tour guide.

....

e Sonia is Italian. Sonia is an interpreter.

....

3 Now make up five statements of your own using some of the following words.

beautiful	good	ugly	cute	dull	handsome
funny	kind	young	silly	sad	good-looking
intelligent	happy	old	boring	evil	unusual
energetic	strange	lonely	exciting	stupid	interesting

4 a **Pair Work** What do these people do?

Descriptions | *Occupations*

I have a boring job. I work in an office, and I do the same things every day. I write letters and I answer the telephone. ....

I have an unusual and exciting job. I travel all over the world. I work with a camera, but I'm not an actor. ....

b **Pair Work** Now describe an occupation and ask your partner to guess what it is.

Self-Check

COMMUNICATION CHALLENGE

PairWork Student A: Look at Challenge 4A on page 114. Student B: Look at Challenge 4B on page 125.

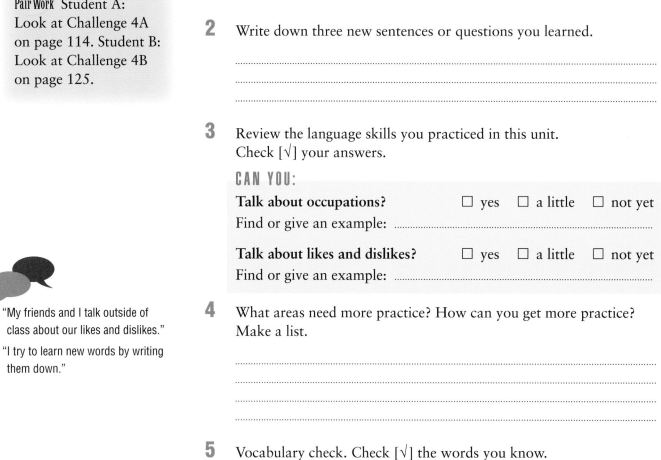

"My friends and I talk outside of class about our likes and dislikes."

"I try to learn new words by writing them down."

1 Write down five new words you learned in this unit.

....

2 Write down three new sentences or questions you learned.

....

....

....

3 Review the language skills you practiced in this unit. Check [√] your answers.

CAN YOU:

Talk about occupations? ☐ yes ☐ a little ☐ not yet

Find or give an example: ....

Talk about likes and dislikes? ☐ yes ☐ a little ☐ not yet

Find or give an example: ....

4 What areas need more practice? How can you get more practice? Make a list.

....

....

....

....

5 Vocabulary check. Check [√] the words you know.

Adjectives			Adverb	Nouns			Quantifier	Verbs
☐ beautiful	☐ exciting	☐ silly	☐ a lot	☐ architect	☐ engineer	☐ painter	☐ much	☐ buy
☐ boring	☐ famous	☐ strange		☐ art	☐ impersonator	☐ professor		☐ impersonate
☐ colorful	☐ good	☐ stupid		☐ computer	☐ lawyer	☐ receptionist		☐ use
☐ cute	☐ handsome	☐ ugly		programmer	☐ music	☐ writer		
☐ dull	☐ rich	☐ young		☐ doctor	☐ musician			
☐ energetic	☐ sad							
☐ evil	☐ selective							

Picture 1

Picture 2

Picture 3

Picture 4

Picture 5

Picture 6

Picture 7

Task 1

How many occupations do you know? Label the pictures.

Task 2

Circle the word that doesn't belong in each line.

a name, address, friend, occupation, nationality
b uncle, father, son, nephew, daughter
c tall, happy, blond, female, handsome
d big, interesting, difficult, easy, boring
e movie, concert, singer, video, album

Task 3

a 🎧 Listen. How many different conversations do you hear?

1   2   3   4   5

b 🎧 Now listen again and fill in the chart.

	NAME	NATIONALITY	OCCUPATION
Conversation 1	Chuck		
Conversation 2	Tomoko		
Conversation 3	George		
Conversation 3	Anita		
Conversation 4	Cynthia		

c Group Work Student A: Keep your book open. Other students: Close your books. Student A: Say a nationality or an occupation. Other students: Make questions like the following ones.

What does .... do?
Where is .... from?

Example: Student A: France.
Student B: Where is Anita from?

Task 4

🎧 Pair Work Listen and fill in the missing information in the form at left.

ENROLLMENT FORM | Pacific Language School

Personal Information
Last name ....
First name .... *Carmen* ....
Citizenship .... *Argentinean* ....
Local address ....
Telephone .... *555-4083* ....
Occupation ....
Employer .... *Aerolineas Argentinas* ....
Highest level of education ....
Passport number .... *E6599139* ....

Language Needs
understand native
speakers
talk to passengers!

Task 5

a Pair Work Ask and answer questions using these cues.

- what / last name
- what / first name
- what / do
- who / work for
- what / qualifications
- where / live
- why / want / study English

b Fill in the following form for your partner.

ENROLLMENT FORM	.... (Name of your school)
Personal Information	*Language Needs*
Last name	....
First name	....
Citizenship	....
Local address	....
Telephone	....
Occupation	
Employer	
Highest level of education	
Passport number	

Task 6

a Pair Work On a piece of paper write the first names of three of the following people: your favorite actor, your father, the person who sits next to you in class, your best friend, your favorite singer, your mother.

b Pair Work Exchange papers and ask questions.

Example: "Who is Paul?" "The person who sits next to me in class."

Task 7

a Think of questions for these answers.

1. She's a student.
2. Oh, yes. I just love English.
3. No, I don't like classical music much—I prefer pop music, actually.
4. New York.
5. I guess they're from Japan.
6. Tony.
7. No, I don't have a sister—but I have three brothers.
8. Who, Anya? Oh, she's an artist. She's really well known.

b Ask and answer the questions.

6 A Place to Stay

Warm-Up

Unit Goals

In this unit you will:

Ask for permission and make requests
"Can I stay with you?"

Talk about ability
"They can both swim."

Talk about quantity
"How many bedrooms are there?"

"How much is the two-bedroom apartment?"

Statement ....

Statement ....

Statement ....

Statement ....

1 Match these statements with the places above.

   a I live in an apartment in Hawaii. We have fabulous views of the ocean.

   b My parents live in a mobile home. They love it.

   c Now, this place should be good for you. It has four bedrooms, two bathrooms, and a study.

   d The Bedouin live in tents in the desert.

2 **Group Work** Discussion. Which of these places would you like to live in? Give reasons.

3 **Group Work** Discussion. Talk about the furniture in your bedroom at home. Compare your room with the bedrooms of other students.

"I have a bed, a dresser, a desk, and two chairs in my room."

Task 1

Read the fax, and answer the questions below.

FACSIMILE TRANSFER

To: Bill Jennings, Pacific Holdings, Hawaii
From: Mary Sellers
Date: Thursday, November 8

Dear Bill,
Our business meeting is confirmed for next Monday, November 12, in Los Angeles. I have booked us rooms at the following hotel:

Beverly Inn
1829 Wilshire Boulevard
Beverly Hills, 90018
Tel: (310) 555-2020
Fax: (310) 555-0486

Looking forward to seeing you again. (And to some warm weather!)
Kind regards,

Mary

Eastern Holdings Ltd. – Park Plaza – Boston – Massachusetts

a Who is the fax addressed to? ....
b Who is it from? ....
c Where are they going to meet? ....
d Why? ....

Task 2

Listen to the four phone conversations. Take the messages.

Task 3

🎧 Now listen to the telephone conversation between Bill and his secretary. Here are the messages for Bill. Which one does his secretary give him?

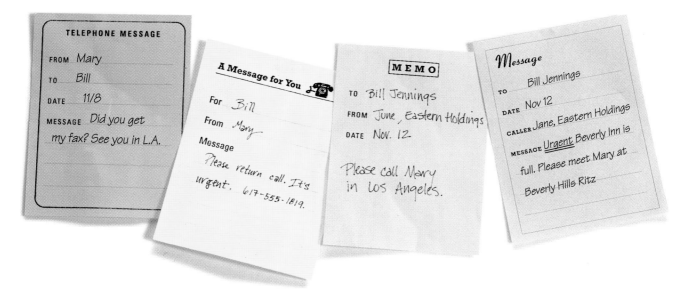

```
TELEPHONE MESSAGE

FROM  Mary
TO    Bill
DATE  11/8
MESSAGE  Did you get
my fax? See you in L.A.
```

```
A Message for You ☎

For    Bill
From   Mary
Message
Please return call. It's
urgent.  617-555-1819.
```

```
MEMO
TO    Bill Jennings
FROM  June, Eastern Holdings
DATE  Nov. 12

Please call Mary
in Los Angeles.
```

```
Message
TO    Bill Jennings
DATE  Nov 12
CALLER Jane, Eastern Holdings
MESSAGE Urgent Beverly Inn is
full. Please meet Mary at
Beverly Hills Ritz
```

Task 4

a 🎧 Pair Work Listen. Bill is talking to a taxi driver in Los Angeles. What is the problem?

b Group Work What can Bill do? Make a list of possibilities.

Example: Perhaps he can stay in another hotel.

Task 5

Read the following letter from Mary. What was the problem?

```
Mr. W. Jennings
Pacific Holdings
1250 Punahou Street
Honolulu, Hawaii

Dear Bill,
I am very sorry about the mix-up in Los Angeles last week.
I want you to know that it was not my fault. The hotel
I booked rooms in changed its name, and the travel agency
gave me the wrong name. Can we meet next week instead?

Sincerely,
Mary
Mary Sellers
```

Language Focus 1 Modal: *can*

1 🎧 Pair Work Listen. Then practice the conversation. Use your own name.

A: Can I speak to Terry, please?
B: Sure. Who's calling?
A: Sally.
B: OK. Wait a minute—I'll get her.
A: Thanks.
C: Terry here.
A: Hi! This is Sally.
C: Hi, Sally!
A: Can I come over and visit?
C: Sure.

2 Ability or requests? Write the number. 1 = ability; 2 = requests/permission.

....*1*.. Can you swim, Tony?
....*2*.. Yes, you can leave the room.
.... Can I speak to Maria?
.... No, you can't stay home today.
.... Maria can speak five languages.
.... Can I smoke in here?
.... They can play tennis really well.
.... You can't leave your bag in the hall.
.... We can come over after school.

3 Pair Work Make requests with *can*.

a You want to speak to Silvia.   *"Can I speak to Silvia, please?"*

b You want to borrow your
   friend's car.   ....

c Your roommate is playing
   music very loudly.   ....

d You want to learn Portuguese
   from Silvia.   ....

e You are visiting a friend and
   want something to drink.   ....

f You want to leave class early.   ....

FIND SOMEONE WHO . . .	NAME
can speak Italian	Tony
can drive a car	

4 Group Work Class survey. Ask classmates questions with *can* and fill in the survey chart at left.

Example: "Can you speak Italian, Tony?" "Yes, I can."

Task Chain 2 Where would you like to live?

LEARNING STRATEGY

Personalizing = sharing your own opinions, feelings, and ideas about a subject.

Task 1

a Complete the following survey.

Where would you like to live?

1. Where do you think is the best place to live?
    a. in the center of the city
    b. in a suburb
    c. in a small town or village
    d. in the country
    e. _____ (other)

2. What sort of place would you like?
    a. a large house
    b. a small house
    c. an apartment
    d. a single room
    e. _____ (other)

3. Who would you like to live with?
    a. alone
    b. with a family
    c. with one friend
    d. with several friends
    e. _____ (other)

4. How much would you like to spend per month?_____

5. What would you like near your house?
    a. a park
    b. a shopping mall
    c. a library
    d. a health club

A Where do you think is the best place to live, Pat?

B I prefer the center of the city.

b GroupWork Survey. Now ask two other students for their opinions.

Task 2

a 🎧 Listen for three people answering the questions in the survey. Write their answers.

	PERSON 1	PERSON 2	PERSON 3
Question 1			
Question 2			
Question 3			
Question 4			
Question 5			

b Who is the most like you? Who is the least like you?

c GroupWork Compare your responses with the responses of three other students.

Room 1

Room 2

Room 3

Task 3

You choose: Do **Ⓐ** or **Ⓑ**.

Ⓐ **Pair Work** What does the word *home* mean to you? Check [√] the following statements and add some of your own.

A home is somewhere . . .

- ☐ I can be safe.
- ☐ I can keep my things.
- ☐ I can have parties.
- ☐ I can take care of my parents/children.
- ☐ I can make a lot of noise.
- ☐ I can invite my friends.
- ☐ ....
- ☐ ....
- ☐ ....

Now compare your statements with another pair's statements.

Ⓑ 🎧 **Pair Work** Listen. Teresa is calling about a room to rent. Which room?

Task 4

a **Group Work** Discussion. Look at the following information. Is any of the information surprising or unusual? Do you think the information would be similar or different in your country? How?

Where do North Americans live?

Houses	57%
Apartments	40%
Other	3%

Who do young North Americans live with?

- 4% of people aged 15 to 24 live alone.
- 25% of people aged 25 to 44 live alone.
- 77% of people aged 18 to 24 have never married.
- 66% of unmarried people aged 18 to 24 live with their parents.

b **Group Work** Discussion. Where do you live? In an apartment? In a house? When do young people usually leave their parents' homes in your country? Do they live alone or with friends? Do young people live together before they get married?

Language Focus 2 *How much? How many?*

1 🎧 **Pair Work** Listen. Then practice the following conversation.

A: I'm calling about the apartment you have for rent.
B: Yes?
A: How many rooms does it have?
B: Five.
A: OK. How many bedrooms does it have?
B: Two.
A: Oh, I want a three-bedroom apartment. How much is the rent?
B: $800 a month.
A: Oh, I'm sorry, that's too much.

2 Number these sentences to make a conversation.

.... Let's see—eight.
.... $700 a month.
.... Well, it has a yard. And there are shops nearby.
.... How much is the rent?
.... What do you want to know?
.... You're welcome.
.... What else does it have?
.... Well, how many rooms does it have?
.... Thank you.
.... Can you tell me about the house?

Do you know the rule?

Circle *can* or *can't* to complete each sentence correctly.

Use *how much* to ask questions about things you **can / can't** count.

Use *how many* to ask questions about things you **can / can't** count.

A Do you live in an apartment or a house?

B I live in a house.

A How many rooms does it have?

B Let's see, six.

3 **Pair Work** Ask and answer questions about these places.

> **To let:**
> Studio Apartment
> One bedroom
> Share bathroom
> Close to shops
> $600 per month
> 555-9192

> Four-bedroom apt./2 bathrooms
> Men or women welcome
> No smokers
> Call Kelly
> $300 per month
> 555-3042

4 **Group Work** Survey. Fill in the first row below. Then ask three other students about their homes and fill in the other rows.

NAME	APARTMENT OR HOUSE	NUMBER OF ROOMS	NUMBER OF BEDROOMS
1. you			
2.			
3.			
4.			

Self-Check

COMMUNICATION CHALLENGE

GroupWork Group A: Look at Challenge 6A on page 116. Group B: Look at Challenge 6B on page 118.

1 Write down five new words you learned in this unit.

....

2 Write down three new sentences or questions you learned.

....

....

....

3 Review the language skills you practiced in this unit. Check [√] your answers.

CAN YOU:

Ask for permission and make requests? ☐ yes ☐ a little ☐ not yet

Find or give an example: ....

Talk about ability? ☐ yes ☐ a little ☐ not yet

Find or give an example: ....

Talk about quantity? ☐ yes ☐ a little ☐ not yet

Find or give an example: ....

"I practice speaking on a cassette tape. Then I listen to myself and find my own mistakes."

"I practice making requests with other students."

4 What areas need more practice? How can you get more practice? Make a list.

....

....

....

5 Vocabulary check. Check [√] the words you know.

Adjectives	Nouns					Quantifiers	Verbs	
☐ alone	☐ ability	☐ bedroom	☐ health club	☐ mobile	☐ table	☐ a lot of	☐ can	☐ personalize
☐ married	☐ apartment	☐ chair	☐ furniture	home	☐ chest of	☐ several	☐ mean	☐ rent
	☐ bathroom	☐ facsimile/	☐ garden	☐ permission	drawers		☐ meet	☐ stay
	☐ bed	fax	☐ house	☐ study				

7 In My Neighborhood

Warm-Up

Unit Goals

In this unit you will:

Ask about and say where things are located

"Where's the supermarket?"

"It's on Fourth Avenue."

"It's next to the bank."

"It's near the subway."

Talk about what people are doing

"I'm watching a movie."

1 Pair Work Look at the picture above and find places where you can . . .

- have lunch
- mail a letter
- catch a bus
- buy a newspaper
- buy traveler's checks
- buy some fruit
- borrow a book
- see a movie

2 Pair Work You are moving to a new neighborhood. Talk about all the things you want nearby.

3 Group Work Discussion. How many different neighborhoods have you lived in? Which did you like best? Why?

A I'd like a health club because I like to work out. What about you?

B I'd like a fast-food restaurant.

A Why?

B Because I love to eat, but I hate to cook.

Task Chain 1 Where's the subway?

Task 1

Circle the word or phrase that doesn't belong.

a on the left, on the hill, on the corner, on the roof
b street, city, avenue, boulevard
c subway, bus stop, airport, taxi
d next to, across from, go to, on top of
e park, museum, church, theater

shops

safe

NEIGHBORHOOD

friends and neighbors

somewhere to come home to

Task 2

a **Group Work** What does the term *neighborhood* mean to you? Build a word map.

b **Group Work** Discussion. Think of the "ideal" neighborhood. What would it look like? What facilities would it have?

Task 3

a 🎧 Listen. Silvia is talking about the sort of neighborhood she would like to live in. Make a list of the things she would like and the things she would not like.

b **Group Work** Share your lists with other students.

c 🎧 Listen to Silvia and Charlie talking about different neighborhoods. Note the advantages and disadvantages.

WOULD LIKE	WOULD NOT LIKE

	ADVANTAGES	DISADVANTAGES
Barker Street		
Beaker Hill		
Kellyville		

d **Pair Work** Now decide which is the best neighborhood for Silvia.

Task 4

a **Pair Work** Silvia finally decides to rent an apartment in the Beaker Hill neighborhood. Here is a map of the neighborhood.

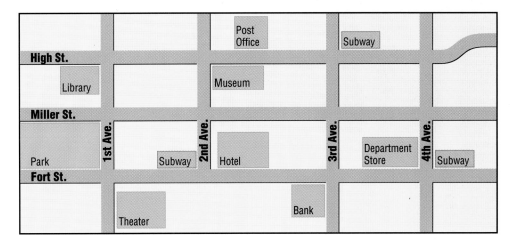

A Is there a museum?

B Yes, there is.

A Where is it?

B It's on the corner of Second Avenue and High Street.

Student A: Ask questions about whether certain places are in the neighborhood, and ask where they are. Use the following words.

museum	post office	hotel	library	park
video store	theater	bank	gym	

Student B: Look at the map and answer the questions.

b **Pair Work** Now change roles and do the task again.

Task 5

Group Work Create your own ideal neighborhood. Make suggestions, and have one student fill in the map.

Example: "There's a pizza parlor on Second Avenue."
"There's a subway on every corner."

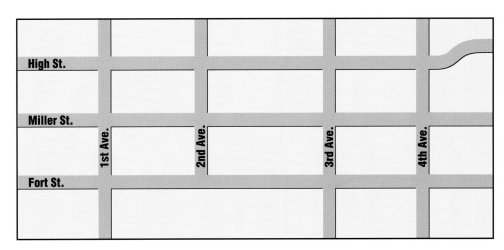

Language Focus 1 Prepositions: *on, next to, near*

1 🎧 Pair Work Listen. Then practice these conversations.

A: Excuse me.
B: Yes?
A: Where's the nearest subway entrance?
B: It's on High Street.
A: And is there a post office anywhere near here?
B: Yes, there's a post office next to the museum.

A: Where's the bank, please?
B: It's on Third Avenue.
A: Thank you.
B: You're welcome.

2 How many statements and questions can you make up from the following words?

| is | post office | Smith Street | where are | it | on |
| and | the | bank | next to | they | |

3 Pair Work Look at the map on page 53 and find the mistakes in the following statements.

a The post office is next to the theater.
b The hotel is on the corner of Fort Street and Fourth Avenue.
c There is a subway on First Avenue.
d The library is near a subway.
e There is a department store on Fourth Avenue.
f The park is on High Street.

Now take turns making correct statements.

Example: "The post office isn't next to the theater. It's next to the museum."

4 Pair Work Look at the map again and answer these questions.

Questions	*Answers*
a Where is the subway?	It's on ....
b Where are the hotel and the department store?	They're on ....
c Where's the museum?	It's next to ....
d Where's the theater?	It's on ....
e Where's the library?	It's near ....

Now talk about where these things are in your own town or neighborhood.

"In my neighborhood, the subway is on 21st Street."

Task Chain 2 Garbage in Hunterville

A What can you do in your neighborhood?

B We can go skating at the Ice Palace.

A What can you buy in your neighborhood?

B Well, you can get good coffee at the Belaroma Café.

A What can you see in your neighborhood?

B There are good movies at the Roseville Cinema.

Task 1

a Think about things you can do, buy, and see in your neighborhood and where. Fill in the chart.

DO	BUY	SEE	WHERE?
ice skating			Ice Palace
	good coffee		Belaroma Café
		movies	Roseville Cinema

b **GroupWork** Ask each other questions about your neighborhoods.

Task 2

a 🎧 Jerry, Mike, and Helen are talking about the good and bad things in their neighborhood. Listen and fill in the chart.

	GOOD	BAD
Jerry		
Mike		
Helen		

b **PairWork** Compare your notes with another student's notes.

Task 3

a **GroupWork** Talk about the things Jerry, Mike, and Helen don't like about their neighborhoods. Suggest possible solutions and list them.

b **GroupWork** Compare your list of solutions with another group's list.

Task 4

Look at the neighborhood picture on page 51. Who lives in this neighborhood—Jerry, Mike, or Helen?

A There's no parking in Helen's neighborhood.

B Maybe they can get better public transportation. Then they won't need cars.

LEARNING STRATEGY

Scanning = searching a text for specific information.

Task 5

a Scan these newspaper articles. Which are problems and which are solutions? Write *P* for problems and *S* for solutions.

b Pair Work Read the articles again and complete the chart.

.... Hunterville: The garbage collection system is so bad that city hall is finally doing something about it. Garbage gets collected late, or not at all. Last month 89 people called to complain about the problem.

.... In response to complaints from residents, city hall is improving facilities in the neighborhood. This year, they are building a pool and a gymnasium. Next year they will build some new sports fields.

.... Police records show that Grantham has the highest crime rate in the whole city. Major crimes include robbery and assault. Car thefts are so common that many people do not bother to lock their cars.

.... In response to complaints from residents, city hall is setting up a new garbage collection and recycling system. The new garbage contractors are putting recycling bins throughout the suburbs so that residents can recycle paper, bottles, and cans.

.... Residents of Newtown are upset because they don't have public transportation. People living in the suburb say that it takes two hours to get to the city by car.

.... We contacted the traffic authority and found that they are developing a new subway system for the suburb. This will cut traveling time to the city by over an hour.

.... Authorities are taking steps to deal with the problems. They are increasing the number of police patrols, and they are establishing a neighborhood watch, a citizen's action organization to watch out for and report crimes.

.... Strathfield: At a town meeting last night, residents complained that they don't have any sports facilities. Their children have to travel several miles to the nearest fitness center. They demanded that the town do something.

PLACE	PROBLEM	SOLUTION
Hunterville	bad garbage collection system	new garbage collection and recycling system

c Pair Work Use the information in the chart to take turns telling about a problem. Your partner will tell about the solution.

Task 6

a Group Work Choose a neighborhood in your city or town and describe it. Make a list of the good and bad things.

NEIGHBORHOOD	GOOD	BAD

b Group Work Compare your list with another group's list.

c Group Work Discussion. Is your city or town doing anything to solve the problems? What is it doing? What do you think it should do?

Language Focus 2 Present progressive for actions in progress

1 🎧 **Pair Work** Listen. Then practice this conversation.

A: Hi, Helen. What are you doing?

B: We're having a neighborhood cleanup.

A: Really? Sounds interesting. What does it involve?

B: Well, we're picking up all the trash, and the kids are painting a mural on that wall, and we're planting some trees along the sidewalk.

A: That's great. Can I help?

B: Sure. You can help Tina. She's emptying that trash can over there.

2 Underline all the progressive verb forms in the following letter.

> Dear Mary,
> I'm having a good time here in New York now that
> I have somewhere to live. As you can see from the photo,
> I'm living in a nice apartment. I had a party last night,
> and most of my friends came. It was great.
>   I'm going out with a nice guy from school, and I'm
> studying hard, so everything is going well.
> Love,
> *Teresa*

Do you know the rule?

Look at the verbs. Then write the rule for changing the base form into the progressive form.

Base Form	Progressive Form
go	going
have	having
be	being
live	living
come	coming
work	working

....
....
....

3 **Group Work** Look at the picture of Helen and Michael above. How many present progressive statements can you make?

Examples: "Michael is talking to Helen."
             "Helen is wearing a T-shirt."

4 **Group Work** Write down what you are wearing at the moment. Give the paper to your teacher. Your teacher will give you a classmate's paper. Read the sentences to the class and guess who wrote them.

Example: "I'm wearing a red jacket and a pair of jeans."

5 **Pair Work** Make statements about your perfect day. Your partner says a time, and you say what you are doing.

Example: "It's 1 p.m." "I'm having lunch with friends."

Self-Check

COMMUNICATION CHALLENGE

Pair Work Student A: Look at Challenge 7A on page 121. Student B: Look at Challenge 7B on page 123.

"I can't remember prepositions. So I draw pictures and stick them on my mirror."

"I'm collecting maps of American cities. I use these to practice directions and locations."

1 Write down five new words you learned in this unit.

....

2 Write down three new sentences or questions you learned.

....

....

....

3 Review the language skills you practiced in this unit. Check [√] your answers.

CAN YOU:

Ask about and say where things are located? ☐ yes ☐ a little ☐ not yet

Find or give an example: ....

Talk about what people are doing? ☐ yes ☐ a little ☐ not yet

Find or give an example: ....

4 What areas need more practice? How can you get more practice? Make a list.

....

....

....

....

5 Vocabulary check. Check [√] the words you know.

Nouns					Prepositions	Verbs		
☐ bus stop	☐ gym	☐ map	☐ neighborhood	☐ subway	☐ near	☐ borrow	☐ mail	☐ sell
☐ church	☐ hotel	☐ museum	☐ park	☐ theater	☐ next to	☐ catch	☐ scan	
☐ department store	☐ library	☐ neighbor	☐ post office		☐ on	☐ hate	☐ see	

8 New York, New York

Warm-Up

Picture 1
Picture 2
Picture 3
Picture 4
Picture 5

Unit Goals

In this unit you will:

Ask about and describe locations of places

"Is there a bookstore around here?"

"There's a bookstore near the subway."

Make, accept, and reject suggestions

"Why don't you go on the boat trip around Manhattan?"

"No, it's too cold today."

"Yes, that's a good idea."

LEARNING STRATEGY

Memorizing conversational patterns and expressions = learning phrases to start conversations and keep them going.

1 Pair Work Match these statements with the places pictured above. What does *it* refer to in each statement?

Pictures	Statements
....	We heard it at Radio City Music Hall.
....	We saw it from the Empire State Building.
....	We did it in Central Park.
....	We saw it in Times Square.
....	We caught it to the Statue of Liberty.

2 a Pair Work How many of these English expressions do you know? Check [√] your answers.

	Yes	Not sure	No
Sorry?	☐	☐	☐
Hi!	☐	☐	☐
See you later.	☐	☐	☐
Excuse me?	☐	☐	☐
See you.	☐	☐	☐
How are you doing?	☐	☐	☐

b Pair Work Which expressions do you use in these situations? Add some situations and have your partner give the correct expressions.

- you are greeting someone
- you are saying goodbye
- you do not understand

Task Chain 1 Making plans

Task 1

a **Group Work** These words describe places. Which words do you know? Circle them.

interesting	small	dirty	exciting
noisy	quiet	beautiful	horrible
crowded	ugly	busy	big
awful	wonderful	expensive	

b **Group Work** Use your dictionary to find unknown words.

Task 2

a **Pair Work** Classify the words in Task 1 into three groups: positive words, negative words, and neutral words.

POSITIVE	NEGATIVE	NEUTRAL
wonderful	awful	interesting

Task 3

Pair Work Can you think of other words to add to the lists?

Task 4

Pair Work Which words would you use to describe your city or neighborhood?

A My neighborhood is noisy and dirty.

B It sounds horrible.

A Yes, but it's also exciting. I like it.

Task 5

🎧 Listen. Pauline and Ron are making plans for the day. Check [√] the words you hear.

- ☐ interesting
- ☐ wonderful
- ☐ noisy
- ☐ beautiful
- ☐ busy
- ☐ nice
- ☐ expensive
- ☐ exciting
- ☐ quiet
- ☐ crowded
- ☐ horrible

SUGGESTIONS	OBJECTIONS

Task 6

a 🎧 **Pair Work** Listen again and note the suggestions and objections in the chart at left.

b What do they finally decide to do?

Task 7

Pair Work Study the following sample guidebook entries. Where can you go to . . .

- entertain your ten-year-old niece?
- eat a late-night meal?
- buy a new compact disc player?
- buy gifts to take home to your parents?

Children's Museum of Manhattan
212 W. 83rd St.
555-5904
The Children's Museum of Manhattan was the idea of Bette Korman, a kindergarten teacher who believed that children needed "laboratories" to explore the world during nonschool hours. The museum is extremely popular, and its newest location now provides even more space for hands-on exhibits.

Lyric High Fidelity
1221 Lexington Ave. (between 82nd and 83rd St.)
555-5710 and 555-1900
Mon.–Wed., Fri., Sat.: 10–6;
Thurs.: 10–8
Lyric is the place for experienced sound fanatics. As Lyric's Michael Kays says, "We're not for beginners, but people who recognize fine equipment and great values can make their dreams come true at Lyric."

Carnegie Delicatessen and Restaurant
854 Seventh Ave. (at 55th St.)
555-2245
There's no other city on earth with delis like New York's, and the Carnegie is one of the best. Its location in the middle of the hotel district makes it the perfect place for midnight snacks. Everything on the menu is made at the deli, and Carnegie offers free delivery between 7 a.m. and 3 a.m. within a five-block area. Remember, come hungry! The sandwiches are huge!

Wanamaker's
1194 Lexington Ave. (between 81st and 82nd St.)
555-2492
Wanamaker's is the place for special household goods. It has unusual household gifts for friends and family—and you'll probably find something for yourself, too!

"I'd take my boyfriend to the Phoenix Restaurant. It's very cheap."

"For an evening of entertainment, we can go to the free concert in the park."

Task 8

Pair Work Talk about places in your own town. Where can you go for . . .

- a meal with your girlfriend/boyfriend/best friend?
- an evening of free entertainment?
- a new car?
- an interesting afternoon with your nine-year-old nephew?

Language Focus 1 Making suggestions with *Why don't you...?*

1 🎧 PairWork Listen. Then practice this conversation with another student.

A: What are you planning to do today?
B: What do you suggest?
A: Why don't you go on the boat trip around Manhattan?
B: No, it's too cold today.
A: Well, why don't you go to a museum or gallery?
B: That's a good idea.

2 PairWork Number these sentences to make a conversation. Then practice the conversation.

.... No, it's too cold.
.... I know what we can do.
.... No, it's too expensive.
.... What can we do this evening?
.... Why don't we go to the new show at Lincoln Center?
.... We can stay home.
.... What?
.... Why don't we go to the free concert in Central Park?

3 PairWork Draw lines to match the suggestions and answers. Then practice them.

Suggestions	*Answers*
a Why don't you visit the gallery?	I'm not hungry.
b Why doesn't he take the subway?	It's too expensive.
c Why doesn't Tomoko go to the theater?	I don't like looking at paintings.
d Why don't we go out to eat?	It's quicker to walk.
e Why don't they stay at the Hilton Hotel?	She doesn't like to go out at night.

4 Make suggestions to someone who asks these questions.

Questions	*Suggestions*
a Are there any good places to take children?	Why don't you .... ?
b All I want to do is eat out somewhere.	Why don't you .... ?
c I need to buy a CD player.	Why don't you .... ?
d I'd like to get something for my sister.	Why don't you .... ?

Task Chain 2 Talking about location

Task 1

Read the paragraph about New York and underline the places and the locations.

Visiting New York

One of the best neighborhoods to stay in for visitors to New York is the Upper East Side. Here, the streets are lined with beautiful town houses, magnificent mansions, and apartment buildings. There are two famous museums (the Guggenheim and the Metropolitan) on Fifth Avenue. There is a famous store (Bloomingdale's) on Lexington Avenue, and there are many mansions on Carnegie Hill. Stop for a cup of coffee or a drink at one of the many cafés and bars on Central Park South. For people who like photography, there is the International Center of Photography on Fifth Avenue. Like most of New York's neighborhoods, the Upper East Side is best seen on foot.

[Source: Adapted from Gerry Frank, *Where to Find it, Buy it, Eat in New York*, Gerry's Frankly Speaking, Salem, Oreg., 1989.]

Task 2

Transfer the information in the text to the chart below.

PLACES	LOCATIONS
famous museums	on Fifth Avenue

Task 3

a 🎧 Listen to Ron talking about his trip to New York. What four things happened to him? Where did they happen?

Incident	*Where*
....	....
....	....
....	....
....	....

b **Pair Work** Compare your answers with another student's answers.

NEW YORK
5082   CENTRAL PARK-NORTH LAKE
G-2465   PHOTOGRAPHER—JON ORTNER

29
USA
Cherokee Strip
Land Run
1893

© 1985 Impact, Glen Burnie, MD 21061
Designed & Distributed in the U.S.A. Printed in Japan

THIS AREA FOR OFFICIAL POSTAL USE ONLY

⊕ RECYCLED PAPER

Task 4

Imagine you are Ron. You are at the airport waiting for your flight. Write a postcard to a friend describing your holiday.

Task 5

a Make a list of all the places you would like to visit in New York. Write down why you would like to visit these places.

Places

....

....

....

Reasons

....

....

....

b **Group Work** Discussion. Talk about the places you would like to visit and say why.

"I come from Bangkok. In Bangkok, there are many interesting Buddhist temples. There's a famous hotel, the Oriental, by the river, and there are lots of jewelry shops on Silom Road."

Task 6

You choose: Do **A** or **B**.

A **Pair Work** List all of the places in your city you would like to show to a visitor. Share your list with another person.

B **Group Work** Discussion. Talk about three famous or interesting places in your city.

Language Focus 2 *There is/there are* and *one, any, some*

1 🎧 **Pair Work** Listen. Then practice this conversation.

A: Is there a bookstore around here?
B: No, there isn't. But there's one near the subway. Why?
A: I want to get a guidebook.
B: Oh, there are some guidebooks on the shelf—help yourself.
A: Thanks a lot.

2 **Pair Work** Fill in the blanks and then practice the questions and answers with another student.

A: .... there a subway near here?
B: Yes, ... is. There's one near the hotel.

A: .... there a restaurant around here?
B: No, there .... , but there's .... in the hotel.

A: .... there any bookstores nearby?
B: Yes, there .... There .... some on Lexington Avenue.

A: .... there .... bars near here?
B: No, there .... But there are .... opposite Central Park.

3 **Pair Work** Look at the guidebook entries on page 61. Make up questions for these answers and then practice them.

Questions	*Answers*
.... ?	Yes, there is. There's one on Seventh Avenue and 55th Street.
.... ?	No, there isn't. But there's one at 212 West 83rd Street.
.... ?	Yes. There's one on Lexington between 82nd and 83rd Streets.
.... ?	Yes. There's one on Lexington between 81st and 82nd Streets.

4 **Pair Work** Write five interesting questions to ask classmates about places in their neighborhood.

5 **Group Work** Survey. Ask other students the questions and write their answers. Share the information with the class.

Self-Check

COMMUNICATION CHALLENGE

Look at Challenge 8 on page 117.

1 Write down five new words you learned in this unit.

....

2 Write down three new sentences or questions you learned.

....

....

....

3 Review the language skills you practiced in this unit. Check [√] your answers.

CAN YOU:

Ask about and describe locations of places?	☐ yes	☐ a little	☐ not yet

Find or give an example: ....

Make, accept, and reject suggestions?	☐ yes	☐ a little	☐ not yet

Find or give an example: ....

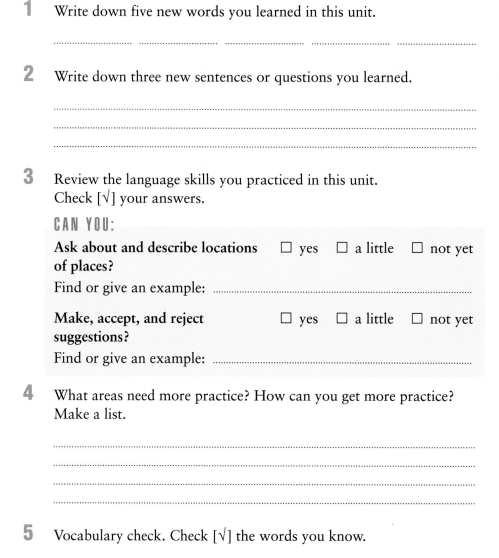

"I have trouble learning grammar. So I choose one grammar point to study every week."

"Sometimes I practice my English at work."

4 What areas need more practice? How can you get more practice? Make a list.

....

....

....

....

5 Vocabulary check. Check [√] the words you know.

Adjectives			Nouns			Quantifiers	Question	Verbs
☐ awful	☐ expensive	☐ quiet	☐ bar	☐ compact	☐ guidebook	☐ any	☐ why	☐ entertain
☐ busy	☐ horrible	☐ small	☐ bookstore	disc	☐ location	☐ one		☐ suggest
☐ crowded	☐ nice	☐ wonderful	☐ café	☐ entertainment	☐ postcard	☐ some		☐ take
☐ dirty	☐ noisy			☐ gift	☐ suggestion			☐ understand
								☐ visit

9 Going Places

Warm-Up

Unit Goals

In this unit you will:

Talk about the weather/climate

"What's the weather like where you come from?"

"It's usually hot in summer."

Ask for and give opinions and advice

"What are the most interesting sights in Barcelona?"

"You should go to Kyoto when you visit Japan."

Caracas ....

London ....

Cairo ....

San Francisco ....

Seoul ....

Barcelona ....

1 Group Work Where are the cities in the pictures above? Write the country names above the pictures.

2 Pair Work Which places would you like to visit? List them in order. Can you give reasons for your choices?

3 a 🎧 Pair Work Listen to Tony and Fabio talking about the temperature, and complete the following:

To convert .... to .... you subtract .... , ... by 5, and .... by 9. To convert .... to .... , you multiply by .... , ... by 5, and add ....

b Complete the table at right.

CELSIUS	FAHRENHEIT
	28
38	

Task 1

a Draw lines to match the words in column A with their opposites in column B.

Column A	Column B
hot	cool
high	cloudy
day	evening
wet	spring
summer	dry
sunny	low
morning	winter
warm	cold
fall	night

b Look at the words in columns A and B. How many of these words can you find in the weather forecasts shown here? Underline them.

Montreal Blue skies; very nice but cool weather continues; high 48, low 35. Tomorrow: Cloudy; morning showers; high 49, low 40.

Los Angeles Sunny; warm readings; high 75, low 58. Tomorrow: Sunny morning; cloudy afternoon; high 72, low 58.

Vancouver Damp and cool with periodic rain; a cold lake breeze; high 49, low 35. Tomorrow: Rain, then showers and sun later; high 56, low 46.

Miami Fine day with sun and mild ocean breezes; high 81, low 69. Tomorrow: Partly sunny; mild night; high, 84, low 70.

Nashville Warm; not as sunny; evening thunderstorm; high 81, low 58. Tomorrow: Partly sunny; showers at night; high 82, low 60.

San Diego After some morning clouds, milder; sunny afternoon; high 71, low 61. Tomorrow: Partly sunny; remaining dry; high 70, low 60.

San Francisco Sunny start, partly cloudy afternoon; high 74, low 56. Tomorrow: Some afternoon rain developing; high 68, low 56.

New York Another beauty—bright and sunny; cloudy night; high 54, low 39. Tomorrow: Cool morning, wet afternoon; high 49, low 43.

[Source: Adapted from *USA Today*.]

Task 2

Group Work Cooperate with two other students. Use the information from Task 1 above to complete the following chart.

CITY	TODAY HIGH	LOW	TOMORROW HIGH	LOW	WEATHER
Montreal	48	35	49	40	*cool, cloudy, showers*
Vancouver					
San Diego					
San Francisco					

Task 3

a Look again at the forecasts in Task 1. Do you think it is spring, summer, fall, or winter? Can you guess what date the forecasts were made? Circle your answer.

February 26   May 14   August 8   November 2

A I like nice weather, so I'd like to be in San Francisco today and San Diego tomorrow.

B Well, I like it warm, so I'd like to be in Miami or Nashville.

b Pair Work Which place would you like to be in today? Which place would you like to be in tomorrow?

Task 4

Write a weather forecast for your town or city.

Task 5

a 🎧 Listen to these weather reports. Which weather words do you hear? Write them in the chart below.

b 🎧 Listen again. Which cities from the forecasts in Task 1 is the announcer talking about? Write them in the chart.

REPORT	WEATHER	CITY
1		
2		
3		

Task 6

Read the following postcard and look at the pictures at the beginning of the unit. Which place is Roger visiting?

Greetings!

July 14

Dear Cynthia,
I'm having a great time. This is an amazing place — you'd love it. The weather is great. It's hot and dry at the moment — the temperature is usually over 100° during the day, and it often reaches 110°. It rarely rains, and even in winter it's usually warm. I hope it's not too cold and wet back home.
Best wishes,
Roger

POSTCARD

Ms. Cynthia Pike
69 Mt. Pleasant
Norwich
Norfolk
England

Task 7

Pair Work Choose a city and write your own postcard as if you're visiting that city. Exchange postcards with a classmate. Can you guess the name of your partner's city?

Language Focus 1 Adverbs of frequency

1 a 🎧 **Pair Work** Listen. Then practice the conversation with another student.

A: What's the weather like where you come from?
B: Well, it's always hot in summer—usually over 40° Celsius.
A: Wow, that's hot. What about winter?
B: It's usually warm in winter. And it hardly ever rains in summer or winter.

b **Pair Work** Now use information that is true for you.

2 **Pair Work** Underline the adverbs of frequency in these statements, and then number them from most frequent *(1)* to least frequent *(6)*.

.... We never go away on long weekends.
.... It often rains when we plan a holiday at the beach.
.... I hardly ever go to parties.
...1... Susie <u>always</u> goes to the beach on the weekend.
.... They sometimes take vacations in winter.
.... He usually goes to the movies on Saturday night.

3 **Pair Work** Draw a line to show where each adverb should go in each sentence.

a Is it warm in the evening?   **usually**
b It is cold in Rio de Janeiro.   **rarely**
c Does it snow in New York?   **often**
d It is wet in London.   **always**
e It snows in Sydney.   **never**

4 a **Pair Work** Take turns talking about how often you do the following things. Use these words in your answers.

never   rarely   sometimes   often

- write letters
- arrive at work/school late
- cook dinner for friends
- sleep with the window open
- stay home on Saturday night
- go away for the weekend
- sing in the shower
- play a musical instrument

b **Group Work** Tell another pair about your partner.

Example: "Tomoko never writes letters."

Do you know the rule?

Complete the statement.

"We usually place adverbs of frequency ....
.... "

Task Chain 2 What should we do on our vacation?

Task 1

Pair Work Where should these people go on vacation? Take turns giving advice.

a Tony loves skiing.   He should *go to Switzerland* .
b Nancy likes Asian art.   She should ....
c Peter studies French.   He should ....
d Sonia is interested in Buddhism. She should ....
e Carmen likes Italian food.   She should ....
f Tomoko studies modern art.   She should ....

Task 2

Group Work Make a list of each person's interests and then decide where he or she should go for vacation.

NAME	INTERESTS	WHERE THEY SHOULD GO
Claudia	the environment, hiking	Nepal or Australia

Task 3

a You are going to listen to a doctor talking about the things you should and shouldn't do when you travel in foreign countries. Before you listen, can you predict some of his advice?

b 🎧 Listen to the doctor's advice and fill in the chart.

THINGS YOU SHOULD DO	THINGS YOU SHOULDN'T DO
take medicine	

c **Pair Work** Do you agree with the doctor's advice? Add your own advice to the list.

d **Group Work** Share your ideas with another pair.

A You know a lot about Japan, don't you?

B I guess so. Why?

A I need some advice. My cousin is visiting Japan next month. She's interested in art and architecture. Where should she go?

B Well, she should definitely visit Kyoto. She should also go to Tokyo.

A We agreed that you should take medicine with you. We disagreed that you shouldn't eat uncooked food.

B We think you should have an emergency health care number you can call.

Task 4

a **Group Work** Choose a city to visit. Then choose five things from the following list to take with you. Give reasons for your choice.

guidebook	bus schedule	money	shopping bag
sunglasses	passport	hat	umbrella
camera	watch	phrase book	map
driver's license	credit card	raincoat	sweater

Example: "I think we should take sunglasses because the weather is going to be nice."

b **Group Work** Can you add more items to the list?

Task 5

a List the three most interesting cities or places in your country and why people should visit them.

City/Place	*Why is it interesting?*
....	....
....	....
....	....

b **Group Work** Share your ideas with three other students.

"You should visit Chiang Mai, in Thailand. It's a beautiful city, and you can visit the hill tribe villages."

Language Focus 2 Modal: *should*

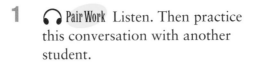

1 **Pair Work** Listen. Then practice this conversation with another student.

A: Where should we go for our vacation?
B: Why don't we go to Mexico?
A: No, we went there last year.
B: You're right. I guess we should go somewhere new.
A: And somewhere interesting.
B: Why don't we go somewhere really different, like Thailand?
A: That's a good idea.

2 **a** **Pair Work** Number these questions and sentences in the correct order to make a conversation. Then practice it.

.... How about the Bahamas?
.... Then why don't you go to Australia?
.... What do you like to do?
.... No. It's too far.
.... Where should I go for my vacation?
.... Well, I like swimming and underwater diving.
.... No, everything is too expensive there.

b **Pair Work** Now have a similar conversation with information that is true for you.

3 **Pair Work** Choose one of the places from the weather forecasts in Task Chain 1. Give some advice for a visitor going to this place. Your partner then can try to guess the name of the city.

A Today you should wear a sweater and a jacket. Tomorrow you should take an umbrella or a raincoat.

B I think that you're talking about Montreal.

4 Write five things someone visiting your city should or shouldn't do. Use these things to talk about your city.

Example: "Well, you shouldn't visit in summer because it's too hot. You should come in spring, because the weather is great then."

....
....
....
....
....

Self-Check

COMMUNICATION CHALLENGE

Look at Challenge 9A on page 119.

1 Write down five new words you learned in this unit.

....

2 Write down three new sentences or questions you learned.

....

....

....

3 Review the language skills you practiced in this unit.
Check [√] your answers.

CAN YOU:

Talk about the weather/climate?   ☐ yes   ☐ a little   ☐ not yet
Find or give an example: ....

Ask for and give opinions and advice?   ☐ yes   ☐ a little   ☐ not yet
Find or give an example: ....

"I buy an English-language newspaper and read about the weather around the world."

"My brother-in-law is Canadian. I practice with him."

4 What areas need more practice? How can you get more practice? Make a list.

....

....

....

....

5 Vocabulary check. Check [√] the words you know.

Adjectives		Adverbs		Nouns				Verbs
☐ cloudy	☐ hot	☐ always	☐ sometimes	☐ advice	☐ evening	☐ passport	☐ temperature	☐ continue
☐ cold	☐ mild	☐ never	☐ there	☐ camera	☐ fall	☐ raincoat	☐ umbrella	☐ give
☐ cool	☐ sunny	☐ often	☐ usually	☐ city	☐ license	☐ spring	☐ watch	☐ know
☐ dry	☐ warm	☐ rarely		☐ country	☐ money	☐ summer	☐ weather	☐ should
☐ high	☐ wet			☐ credit card	☐ month	☐ sunglasses	☐ winter	
				☐ day	☐ night	☐ sweater		

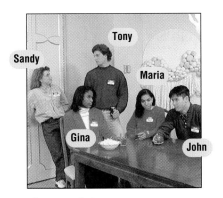

Photograph A

Photograph B

Task 1

a Pair Work Student A: Look at photograph A. Student B: Look at photograph B. How many differences can you find? Make statements like these:

Tony .... is standing up.
.... is sitting down.
.... is next to ....
.... is near the ....
.... is drinking a soda.
.... is eating a sandwich.
.... is eating an apple.
.... is wearing a .... sweater.

b Pair Work Make a list of all the differences you found.

c Group Work Now compare your list with another pair's list. Who found the most differences?

Task 2

Classify the following words.

interesting	usually	rarely	crowded	on
often	exciting	quiet	near	always
expensive	next to	sometimes	beautiful	never

Words You Can Use To . . .

SAY HOW OFTEN THINGS HAPPEN	DESCRIBE PLACES OR THINGS	SAY WHERE THINGS ARE LOCATED
usually	interesting	on

Dear John,
Miami is a fabulous place.
The weather is great — it's
always warm and it's usually
sunny. There's lots to do
too — I'm sitting on the beach
at the moment, enjoying the
sun. You should come and visit
me sometime.
Love,
Tina

© FLYING FISH, INGLEWOOD

Task 3

a Talk about your favorite city.

Example: "Well, I just love San Francisco. The climate is good, although it's a little cool in winter. It's very pretty, and there's lots to do."

b Now study the model at left, and write a postcard about your favorite city.

Task 4

a 🎧 **Pair Work** Listen. Then practice this conversation with another student.

A: Hi, Maria, what are you doing?
B: Nothing much—just watching TV.
A: I'm not doing anything special either. Why don't we go to a movie?
B: No, not tonight. I'm tired.
A: Oh, that's what you always say.
B: Yes, I'm always tired when you call.

b **Pair Work** Change roles and practice the conversation again.

Task 5

Pair Work Draw lines to match the two parts of the conversations, and then circle the correct verb form in the second part of each conversation. Practice the questions and answers with another student.

1. Can I speak to Sally?
2. What does Paul do?
3. Where does Sandy go to school?
4. What is John doing?

5. He **tries / is trying** to study.
6. She **goes / is going** to UCLA.
7. I'm sorry—she's not home. She **shops / is shopping.**
8. He **is / is being** a student.

11 Time Out

Warm-Up

Photograph 1

Unit Goals

In this unit you will:

Discuss hobbies and leisure activities

"What do you do in your spare time?"

"I play the guitar."

Ask and tell about past events

"What did you do over the weekend?"

"I went to the movies."

Describe a sequence of events

"I had a great time over the weekend. First I played tennis, then I went out to dinner, and then I went to the movies."

A I like sleeping late and having fun over the weekend.

B Unfortunately, I have to clean the house over the weekend.

Photograph 2

Photograph 3

Photograph 4

Photograph 5

Photograph 6

Photograph 7

1 **Pair Work** Look at the photos above. How many of these activities can you name?

2 **a** **Group Work** What do you usually do on the weekend? Brainstorm and write down all the words and phrases you can think of.

b **Group Work** Now talk about your weekend activities.

Task 1

Look at this list of hobbies. Which hobbies do you do? Which would you like to do? Check [√] your answers.

	Do	Would like to do
cook Chinese food	☐	☐
gardening	☐	☐
play chess	☐	☐
go whale watching	☐	☐
play the guitar	☐	☐
race cars	☐	☐
play golf	☐	☐
watch movies	☐	☐
watch birds	☐	☐
fly model airplanes	☐	☐

A Well, I think it's usually young men who race cars.

B I agree that it's often young people who race cars, but I think it's not just men—women race cars, too.

Task 2

Pair Work Pick three or four hobbies. What sort of person likes these hobbies? (Specify ages, men or women, children or adults, etc.)

Task 3

a **Pair Work** Look at these statements. What hobbies do they refer to? Which words helped you guess?

	Hobbies	Keywords
I grew some beautiful roses last year.	gardening	grew, roses
I tried out my new set of clubs.	....	....
We need more rice and soy sauce.	....	....
I broke another string last night.	....	....
Jack Nicholson was the best actor in it.	....	....
Make sure you cut off the dead flowers.	....	....
Could I borrow your binoculars?	....	....

b **Pair Work** Take turns making statements like the ones above and guessing which hobbies your partner is thinking about.

Task 4

🎧 Listen to Sophie, Teresa, and Ken talking about their weekends. Which hobbies from Task 1 do you hear? Circle them.

Task 5

🎧 Listen again, and look at these pages from a daily planner. Who wrote each entry?

Name ....

SATURDAY
29
JAN. 1994

DECEMBER
FEBRUARY

7:00
7:30
8:00 shopping / laundry
8:30 pay rent!
9:00
9:30
10:00
10:30
11:00 lunch
11:30 gardening with Mom
12:00
1:00
1:30
2:00
2:30
3:00
3:30
4:00
4:30
5:00

Sunday
- play with Mark — chess?
- lunch (pizza!)
- shopping
- movies

Name ....

MAY

"When you aim for perfection, you discover it's a moving target."
— GEORGE FISHER

REMEMBER !!! **THURSDAY 28**
PICK UP SAM !!!
— Whale watching /
don't forget
binoculars!
FRIDAY 29

Name ....

Task 6

a Group Work Discussion. Here are the three most popular and three least popular weekend activities in the United States. Guess which three are the most popular and which three are the least popular.

- going fishing
- visiting friends or relatives
- seeing a play
- running errands
- exercising, jogging, walking, or biking
- going to a sporting event

b Group Work Discussion. What do you think are the most and least popular weekend activities in your country?

Language Focus 1 Simple past: statements and yes/no questions

1 🎧 Pair Work Listen. Then practice the conversation with another student using information that is true for you.

A: What did you do over the weekend, Pete?
B: Well, on Saturday, I played golf, and then I went shopping. After that, I worked in the yard. On Sunday, I ran a marathon. What about you?
A: Well, on Saturday, I read a book. After that I took a nap. On Sunday, I watched videos and listened to music.

2 Make simple-past questions from these cues.

Cues	Questions
a you / see / the doctor / yesterday	*Did you see the doctor yesterday?*
b you / go out / last night	....
c he / do / anything special / weekend	....
d they / see / their / friend / on / weekend	....
e they / meet you / movies / last night	....
f we / get / invitation to / party	....

3 Pair Work Study the conversation and discover the spelling rule for the simple past tense of these verbs.

stay   watch   talk   play   work   visit   listen   want

A: I stayed home last night.
B: Oh, yeah? What did you do?
A: I watched the basketball game on TV. What about you?
B: I stayed in and listened to music.

LEARNING STRATEGY

Discovering = finding patterns in language.

4 Circle the word that doesn't belong in each line.

a called, saw, looked, rented
b went, cooked, started, talked
c studied, walked, climbed, happened
d was, wanted, did, had

A Did you go to the movies this weekend, Eric?

B No, I didn't. I went to a concert, though.

5 Group Work Ask some other students about their weekend activities.

Task Chain 2 A wild time!

Task 1

Group Work You are going to hear a story containing these phrases. What do you think it is about?

wild time . . . . won $5,000 . . . . crazy rock station . . . . identify the songs . . . . win $5,000 . . . . took Jerry and Kay out to dinner . . . . went to the theater . . . . went to that new disco . . . . danced all night . . . . took a limo home . . . . crashed into bed . . . . next morning . . . . no money . . . .

Task 2

🎧 Listen to the conversation and circle the words that are different from the ones you hear.

a I had a really wonderful time yesterday.
b You won five thousand?
c Well, there's this crazy pop station, and every hour they invite people to call in.
d I took Terry and Kay out to lunch to celebrate.
e Then we went to the movies.
f Then I took a taxi home.
g I fell into bed.
h Did you contact the police?
i I went back to sleep.
j We might have spent it all the night before.

Task 3

🎧 Listen again and number these pictures in the order each event happened.

Picture ....

Picture ....

Picture ....

Picture ....

Picture ....

Picture ....

Picture ....

Task 4

a GroupWork Work with three or four other students. What happened to the money? Make a list of possibilities. Which group has the most interesting or unusual list?

b GroupWork Discussion. What would you do in this situation? Has anything like this ever happened to you?

Task 5

PairWork Retell the story in your own words.

Task 6

a Number these sentences to make a story.

.... However, the limo company owners said that no one had reported any missing money.

.... They told him that if no one claimed the money in a week he could keep it.

.... He counted it and found that the bundle came to $2,500.

.... Next, he went to the police, but they said the same thing.

.... Of course, the first thing he did was to go to the limo company to return the money.

.... No one claimed the money, so Jimmy was able to keep it.

.... Last week he found a large bundle of money under the seat of a limo he was riding in.

.... Jimmy Garcia is a little richer this morning.

b PairWork Write a title for the story. ....

Language Focus 2 Simple past: connecting words and *wh* questions

1 🎧 **Pair Work** Listen. Then practice the conversation.

A: What did you do on your vacation, Sandra?
B: Oh, I had a great time. I did lots of different things.
A: Where did you go?
B: Well, first I went hiking in Nepal, and then I went scuba diving in Australia. Finally, I went skiing in Switzerland.
A: Wow, it sounds like you had a great time.

2 a **Pair Work** Fill in the blanks with four of these connecting words.

then   after that   next   first   finally

A: Oh, great, it's working again.
   How did you fix it?
B: Well, ... I checked to see
   if there was a cassette inside.
   .... I reread the instructions.
   .... I called my repair shop.
   .... , I discovered that it
   wasn't plugged in!

b What kind of machine are these instructions for?

3 **Pair Work** Fill in the blanks and then practice the questions and answers.

A: What .... you do Saturday night?
B: .... I had dinner, and .... I watched a video.

A: Where .... she go on Friday?
B: .... she went to school, and .... she visited friends.

A: What did he .... last night?
B: .... he .... dinner, ... he .... with a friend, and .... they saw a movie. .... he .... home and .... to bed.

4 a **Pair Work** Each of you will tell a story containing four events. Take notes on your partner's story here:

First, ...
Then, ...
Next, ...
Finally, ...

b **Pair Work** Ask *wh* questions about your partner's story.

Example: "Where did it happen? When did it happen?"

Self-Check

COMMUNICATION CHALLENGE

GroupWork Student A: Look at Challenge 11A on page 120. Student B: Look at Challenge 11B on page 122. Student C: Look at Challenge 11C on page 124.

"I try to write something in English every day."

"I memorize lists of past-tense verb forms."

1 Write down five new words you learned in this unit.

....

2 Write down three new sentences or questions you learned.

....

....

....

3 Review the language skills you practiced in this unit. Check [√] your answers.

CAN YOU:

Discuss hobbies and leisure activities?   □ yes   □ a little   □ not yet

Find or give an example: ....

Ask and tell about past events?   □ yes   □ a little   □ not yet

Find or give an example: ....

Describe a sequence of events?   □ yes   □ a little   □ not yet

Find or give an example: ....

4 What areas need more practice? How can you get more practice? Make a list.

....

....

....

5 Vocabulary check. Check [√] the words you know.

Connecting Phrases and Words

□ after that   □ first   □ then
□ finally   □ next

Nouns

□ chess   □ guitar   □ taxi
□ coffee shop   □ hobby   □ weekend
□ discovering   □ instructions   □ whale
□ flowers   □ leisure
□ game   □ roses

Verbs

□ clean   □ hang   □ skiing
□ cooked   gliding   □ sleep
□ did   □ ran   □ was
□ discover   □ saw   □ watch
□ fly   □ scuba   □ went
  diving   □ were

12 HOLLYWOOD
That's Entertainment

Warm-Up

Picture 1

Picture 2

Picture 3

Picture 4

Picture 5

Picture 6

Unit Goals

In this unit you will:

Talk about entertainment plans

"What are you doing tonight?"

"I'm going to the movies. What about you?"

Express opinions about entertainment

"That's a very boring movie."

1 a Group Work Think about the word *entertainment*. Brainstorm with three or four other students and write down all the words and phrases you can think of.

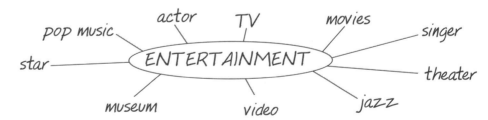

pop music — actor — TV — movies — singer

star — ENTERTAINMENT — theater

museum — video — jazz

b Group Work Which words go together? Can you classify them?

2 a Look at the pictures above. Do you know where the photographs were taken? Write the picture numbers in the blanks beside the correct descriptions.

.... a late-night jazz club   .... a street market

.... a zoo   .... the movies

.... a theater   .... a museum for kids

b Group Work Which places would you like to go to? Compare your choices with other students' choices.

A I'd like to go to the kid's museum.

B You're not a kid.

A I know, but it looks like fun.

This Weekend at the
I-70 Speedway
**The Down-Home
Fall Country
Spectacular**
Featuring
**Andy Walker and the
Range Rovers** and
Wayne "Cowboy" Wilkins
Saturday, Nov. 12, 2 – 8 p.m.
Tickets $18.50/$12.50
For information call 555-9922

The City Symphony Orchestra
will perform
Rosowsky's Requiem
Friday, November 11, 8 p.m.
Tickets $18.50/$12.50

The Metropolitan Ballet Company
presents
Oksana Svetlana & Jonathan Wolf
dancing in
Tchaikovsky's *Imelda*
Friday, November 11, 8 p.m.
Tickets $18.50/$12.50 555-2138

The First Baptist Congregation
presents for one night only
The Mighty Rivers of Joy
Sunday, November 13, 1 p.m.
Tickets $18.50/$12.50
For information call 555-9922

The National Opera Company
Featuring Solo Tenor Antonio DeAngelis
presents Carla's *The Shoemaker of Parma*
Friday, November 11, 8 p.m.
Tickets $18.50/$12.50 555-9834

The Vaishali Modern Dance Project presents
"The night the laundry died"
At the Atherton Theater
Saturday, November 11, 8 p.m.
Tickets $22.50 call 555-7896

The 20th Century Club presents
Every Evening from 8.30 to 12:30
Ballroom Dancing
to the music of Jeffrey "Topcat"
Henderson and his Orchestra
Admission $7

DOWNSTAIRS
AT ERIC'S
LIVE JAZZ
UNTIL DAWN
NO COVER
CHARGE

The Underground Rock Club
The Invisible Jackets with
special guests RocketHead
Friday, November 11, 8 p.m.
Tickets $18.50

Task 1

a Look at these advertisements and rate them according to this scale.

1 = I would love to go.   2 = I would like to go.
3 = I wouldn't like to go.   4 = I would hate to go.

.... country music festival   .... classical music
.... opera   .... hot gospel group
.... ballroom dancing   .... modern dance group
.... late-night jazz club   .... rock concert
.... ballet   .... musical

b Group Work Compare your ratings with the ratings of three other students.

Task 2

a Pair Work Each of these people is going out with one other person tonight. Try to match each person with the person he or she is going out with.

Eva    David    Kiti

b 🎧 Listen to the answering machine messages and write the correct responses in the blanks.

John is going out with ....
Kiti is going out with ....
Eva is going out with ....

Task 3

a Pair Work look at the advertisements in Task 1. Where do you think each pair is going tonight?

b 🎧 Listen to the telephone conversations and write the correct responses in the blanks.

Harvey and John are going to ....
David and Kiti are going to ....
Lorraine and Eva are going to ....

c Group Work Find out where your classmates are going tonight.

Task 4

a Pair Work These people are coming to town to visit you. Where will you take them?

- your uncle
- your 12-year-old niece
- your older brother
- a very close friend

b Compare your choices with another pair's choices.

Task 5

You have been to one of the events in Task 1. Write a letter to a friend describing it.

John

Lorraine

Harvey

Language Focus 1 Present progressive for planned future

1 🎧 Pair Work Listen. Then practice this conversation with another student.

A: Hi, Artie. What are you doing tonight?
B: I'm going to the movies.
A: What are you seeing?
B: *Blade Runner.*
A: But that came out years ago. Haven't you seen it yet?
B: Yes, I've seen it five times before. I love it.

2 Pair Work How many questions can you make from the following words?

where	are	you	what	Tom
going	seeing	tomorrow	tonight	who

3 Pair Work Complete these conversations and practice them.

A: .... are you doing on Saturday?
B: Nothing much. I .... home and .... a book.

A: .... are you seeing tonight?
B: I .... Artie and Julie. We're .... to a movie.

A: .... movie are you seeing?
B: We're .... an old Humphrey Bogart movie.

A: .... are you taking your next vacation?
B: We .... to Hawaii at Christmas.

4 Group Work Ask and answer these questions. Then think of some questions of your own.

a What are you doing next New Year's Eve?
b What are you doing next Sunday?
c Where are you going on your next vacation?
d What is the next movie you are going to see?
e Who are you seeing tomorrow?
f What are you buying next time you go shopping?

Task Chain 2 Out and about

Review 1

This is a rather boring movie from Megafilms about two bank robbers who get away with money and murder—and some fairly bad acting. Eventually they are caught in a small western town, which looks like every small western town in every small western movie ever made. A complete waste of time!

A middle-aged art critic becomes friendly with a young woman who is in a difficult relationship with a famous artist. Eventually she realizes that the critic is more sensitive and creative than the selfish boyfriend. The film is about the woman's inner struggle to break free from the power of her boyfriend and her fear of falling in love with the art critic. Highly recommended.

Review 2

This film was made for children, although parents may enjoy it as well. Four young children get locked in a Disney-type theme park overnight. When the sun goes down, all the creatures in the park come to life. Corny? Perhaps. But the young actors' remarkable performances make the movie well worth seeing.

Review 3

Shakespeare might like this film—or at least be flattered—because the plot has been stolen from several of his plays. A jazz musician strangles his wife to the music of the Phil Gould Big Band. Of course, the murderer gets caught in the end, but not before boring the audience to death. This movie should be shown only on airplanes. See it if you must.

Review 4

Task 1

a Pair Work Think of an example of each of these types of movies.

Thriller: ....
Horror: ....
Comedy: ....
Romance: ....
Drama: ....
Adventure: ....
Western: ....

b Group Work Compare your answers with those of another pair.

Task 2

a Write brief answers to these questions.

Questions	Answers
Do you often go to the movies?	....
What is your favorite type of movie?	....
What are your five favorite movies?	....
	....
	....
	....
	....

b How do you usually decide which movie to see?
Check [√] your responses.

☐ I ask my friends.
☐ I read movie reviews.
☐ I look at movie advertisements.
☐ I watch previews.

c Group Work Discuss your responses with three other students.

Task 3

a Match the movie titles below with the reviews at left. Write the number of each review in the blank before the correct title.

.... *Creatures From the Past*
.... *The Power of Love*
.... *With These Hands*
.... *Wild Horses*

b **Pair Work** Look at the list of film types in Task 1. Decide what type of film each of these is. Are the reviews positive or negative (good or bad)? Complete the chart.

TITLE	TYPE OF MOVIE	REVIEW

Task 4

a 🎧 Listen to these people talking about the movies. Check [√] the phrases you hear.

- ☐ very exciting
- ☐ too long
- ☐ pretty boring
- ☐ very interesting
- ☐ really good
- ☐ not too interesting

b 🎧 Now listen again and look at the reviews in Task 3. Which movie is each person talking about? Do the people agree or disagree with the reviews?

CONVERSATION	FILM TITLE	AGREE / DISAGREE
1		
2		
3		
4		

Task 5

Write a review of your favorite movie.

Language Focus 2 — Intensifiers: *too, fairly, pretty, very*

1 🎧 **Pair Work** Listen. Then practice this conversation with another student.

A: Where do you want to go?
B: Well, it's too cold to stay outdoors.
A: Why don't we go to the movies? There's one at the Showcase Cinema that sounds pretty interesting.
B: What is it?
A: *Wild Horses.*
B: Oh, with Kurt Russell. He's a very good actor. OK, let's go.

2 How many words can you delete from these questions and sentences?

a There is a very good movie at the Odeon.
   There is a movie at the Odeon.

b Is there a very good movie on right now?
   ....

c I saw a really boring show on TV last night.
   ....

d Michelle Pfeiffer is a really good actress.
   ....

e That movie is too old.
   ....

f Those are pretty funny programs.
   ....

3 **Pair Work** Discuss famous entertainers, TV shows, movies, and songs. How many statements and questions can you make from these cues?

a *I think talk shows are just* .... too boring.
b .... a very exciting ....
c .... pretty old ....
d .... a fairly interesting ....

A I'm thinking of a movie.
B Is it very exciting?
A Yes, it is.
C Is it fairly new?
A No, it isn't.
D Is it *Home Alone?*
A No, it isn't.
B Was it shown on TV fairly recently?
A Yes, it was.
C Is it *Rear Window?*
A Yes, it is.

4 **Group Work** Take turns thinking of a movie, TV show, actor, or singer. State the category. The other students will ask you questions with *yes* or *no* answers to try to guess what you are thinking of. Answer each question only if it contains one of these words: *too, fairly, pretty, very.*

Self-Check

COMMUNICATION CHALLENGE

PairWork Student A: Look at Challenge 12A on page 114. Student B: Look at Challenge 12B on page 127.

"I read the entertainment pages of English-language newspapers."

"I watch English-language videos and sing songs in English."

1 Write down five new words you learned in this unit.

....

2 Write down three new sentences or questions you learned.

....

....

....

3 Review the language skills you practiced in this unit. Check [√] your answers.

CAN YOU:

Talk about entertainment plans? ☐ yes ☐ a little ☐ not yet
Find or give an example: ....

Express opinions about entertainment? ☐ yes ☐ a little ☐ not yet
Find or give an example: ....

4 What areas need more practice? How can you get more practice? Make a list.

....

....

....

....

5 Vocabulary check. Check [√] the words you know.

Adjectives		Adverbs	Nouns				Verbs	
☐ classical	☐ long	☐ fairly	☐ adventure	☐ jazz	☐ preview	☐ star	☐ classify	☐ enjoy
☐ creative	☐ selfish	☐ free	☐ club	☐ modern	☐ review	☐ thriller	☐ decide	☐ go out
☐ gospel	☐ sensitive	☐ pretty	☐ comedy	dance	☐ romance	☐ zoo		
			☐ critic	☐ opera				

13 Healthy Living

Warm-Up

1 *GroupWork* Look at the two photographs. What differences can you find?

2 *GroupWork* Compare these differences with those found by another group.

Example: "In the first photo, some people are drinking beer and wine. In the second, they're drinking juice."

3 Check [√] those things in the picture that you think are healthy. Put an [X] next to the things that are unhealthy.

4 Think about your habits over the last month. Check [√] your responses.

Have you . . .	*Yes*	*No*	*Don't remember*
▪ stayed up past one o'clock in the morning?	☐	☐	☐
▪ played any sports?	☐	☐	☐
▪ done some other kinds of physical activity?	☐	☐	☐
▪ eaten junk food?	☐	☐	☐
▪ drunk alcohol?	☐	☐	☐
▪ smoked?	☐	☐	☐

5 *PairWork* Take turns asking and answering the questions in the previous activity.

Unit Goals

In this unit you will:

Talk about past experiences

"Have you ever been hang gliding?"

"Yes, I have."

"No, I haven't."

Talk about how often things happen

"How often do you exercise?"

"About three times a week."

A Have you stayed up past one o'clock in the morning?

B Yes, I have.

C No, I haven't.

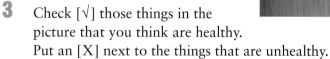
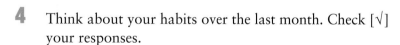
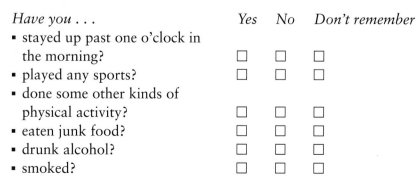

Task Chain 1 Talking about sports

Task 1

a Draw lines to match the symbols with the sports.

golf   baseball   swimming   ice hockey   tennis   skiing   soccer   volleyball   running

A Have you ever played golf?

B Yes, I have.

b **Pair Work** Ask your partner which sports he or she has played.

Task 2

Pair Work How well do you know these sports? Fill in the chart.

DESCRIPTION	GOLF	SOCCER	RUNNING	BASEBALL	SKIING	VOLLEYBALL
Uses a ball	yes	yes	no	yes	no	yes
Is a team sport						
Is played outdoors						
Is played indoors						
Is played in winter						
Is played in summer						
Is played on a court						

A This sport uses a ball. It's a team sport, and it's played outdoors.

B Is it played on a court?

A No, it isn't.

C Is it soccer?

A No, it isn't.

B Is it baseball?

A Yes, it is.

Task 3

Group Work Tell about a sport. Have your classmates try to guess the sport.

Task 4

🎧 Listen to three people talking about their favorite sports. Can you guess the sports? Which words helped you guess? Fill in the chart.

PERSON	SPORT	KEYWORDS
1		
2		
3		

Task 5

a PairWork Where do you think accidents happen? Write your guesses in the chart.

Example: "I think 50% of accidents happen in the home, for both men and women."

Where People Have Accidents

		OUR GUESS	NEWSPAPER INFORMATION
At Work	Men	%	%
	Women	%	%
Playing Sports	Men	%	%
	Women	%	%
At Home	Men	%	%
	Women	%	%
On the Road	Men	%	%
	Women	%	%

"We guessed that 20% of injuries to women happen at work. In the report, it says that 11.2% of injuries to women happen at work."

b PairWork Now read the newspaper report and complete the chart. Compare your guesses with the newspaper information.

Americans are having more accidents these days. Between 1983 and 1990, the proportion of people injured in accidents rose from 7% to 13%. Over 2,800,000 accidents have been studied so far. Of these, 26.5% of men and 23.8% of women said they had an illness or injury attributable to an accident that occurred during sports, recreation, or exercise. Among men, 27.7% of accidents occurred at work, while for women the figure for accidents at work was 11.2%. Among women, 38.4% reported that their accidents occurred at their home or at the home of a friend or relative. For men, the figure for accidents at home was 30.5%. The final category included accidents that occurred on a sidewalk, road, or highway. Here the figure for men was 15.3%, compared with 26.06% for women.

Task 6

PairWork Which of these headlines would you use for the article?

Women Are Healthier Than Men
Number of Accidents on the Rise
Get Less Exercise
Women Have Fewer Accidents Than Men

Language Focus 1 Present perfect and *Have you ever...?*

1 a 🎧 **Pair Work** Listen. Then practice the conversation.

A: Have you ever been hang gliding?
B: No, I haven't. Have you?
A: Yes, I have.
B: What's it like?
A: It's great.
B: Have you ever had an accident?
A: Unfortunately, yes.

b **Pair Work** Now use information that is true for you.

2 **Pair Work** Make up questions for these answers and then practice them.

	Questions	*Answers*
a	.... ?	No, she hasn't. It's too dangerous.
b	.... ?	No, I haven't. I don't have a license.
c	.... ?	No, he hasn't. He doesn't like high places.
d	.... ?	No, they haven't. They aren't old enough.
e	.... ?	No, we haven't. It's too expensive.

FIND SOMEONE WHO HAS . . .	NAME
driven a racing car	
been to a Grand Prix race	
played squash	
run a marathon	
had music lessons	
ridden a motorcycle	
flown an airplane	
been to a bullfight	
been scuba diving	
played tennis	

3 **Pair Work** Draw lines to match the verb tenses.

Simple Past	*Past Participle*
was	gone
came	taken
did	been
drank	gotten
drove	come
went	spoken
got	known
had	drunk
knew	seen
saw	done
spoke	driven
took	had

4 a Look at this survey chart above and add three activities to the list.

b **Group Work** Now go around the class and collect as many names as you can.

Task Chain 2 — Talking about habits

Task 1

What does the phrase *healthy living* mean to you? How many words can you add to these lists?

Healthy Living

EAT	DO	DRINK	AVOID
whole-grain bread	yoga	fresh fruit juice	tobacco

"I hate whole-grain bread."

"I love fresh fruit juice."

"I think yoga is boring."

"I have never used tobacco products."

Pair Work Now make statements using the words from the lists.

Fitness Index

HABITS	POINTS	HABITS	POINTS
Eats red meat		**Walks**	
every day	1	every day	6
3–5 times a week	2	3–5 times a week	5
once a week	3	once a week	4
once a month	4	once a month	3
3–5 times a year	5	3–5 times a year	2
never	6	never	1
Eats vegetables		**Plays sports or does exercises**	
every day	6	every day	6
3–5 times a week	5	3–5 times a week	5
once a week	4	once a week	4
once a month	3	once a month	3
3–5 times a year	2	3–5 times a year	2
never	1	never	1
Drinks alcohol		**Smokes cigarettes or cigars**	
every day	1	every day	1
3–5 times a week	2	3–5 times a week	2
once a week	3	once a week	3
once a month	4	once a month	4
3–5 times a year	5	3–5 times a year	5
never	6	never	6

Task 2

You choose: Do **A** or **B**.

A **Group Work** Think about the last time you went grocery shopping. Make a list of all the things you bought. Compare this list with the lists of three or four other students. Whose list is the healthiest?

B **Group Work** Think about all the healthy things you did last week. Make a list. Compare this list with the lists of three or four other students. Who had the healthiest week?

Fitness Index Scoring Key

30–36 points: *Excellent* You're in great shape.

13–29 points: *Average* You're in average shape, but you need to be careful.

6–12 points: *Poor* You should change your habits.

Task 3

🎧 Listen to three people talking about their eating and exercise habits. Figure out their fitness indexes using the table on page 97. Record their scores and health ratings in this chart.

PERSON	SCORE	HEALTH RATING
1		
2		
3		

Task 4

a **Pair Work** Interview each other and figure out your fitness index.

b **Pair Work** Do you disagree with any of the scoring in the table?

Example: "I disagree that eating red meat every day is unhealthy. I eat red meat every day and look at me!"

Task 5

a **Group Work** Discussion. Read this section of a newspaper article. What did Gina do that was healthy? What was unhealthy? Is Gina basically a healthy person? Do you like weekends like Gina's? Why or why not?

A How often do you eat red meat?

B Oh, once a week, I guess.

The Single Life: Weekend Profiles

Gina Giorcelli is single and loves it. "I had a great time this weekend," she reports. Gina lives in San Diego, just 15 minutes from the beach. After a busy week, she was ready to relax on Friday night. The weekend started when she met friends for drinks at The Elephant Bar. "I'm not a big drinker, but I had three beers on Friday." They then went to B.J.'s Pizzeria where Giorcelli had a salad. She eats at B.J.'s about three times a month. Saturday morning she helped a friend move to a new house and then did the weekend shopping. In the afternoon she went to her weekly aerobics class. On Saturday evening, Giorcelli had cocktails at a friend's house and a pasta dinner at The Spot. Next she went to the Red Onion, where she danced until 4:00 a.m. She loves dancing and goes to a disco every Saturday night. On Sunday, she got up at 10 and went to a sushi bar for brunch. She spent Sunday afternoon at the beach swimming and playing volleyball, and then she had a fast-food meal. Finally, she walked down Seventh Street to the Mall for the San Diego Folk Festival. "How often do I have such a great weekend? Oh, every weekend."

Language Focus 2 Time expressions and *How often . . . ?*

1 a 🎧 **Pair Work** Listen. Then practice this conversation.

A: How often do you play sports, Pete?
B: Never.
A: And what about exercise? How often do you exercise?
B: Oh, about once or twice a year.
A: Once or twice a year?
B: Yeah. Usually once or twice during the summer I walk down to the park to watch a ball game.

b Pair Work Now use information that is true for you.

2 Pair Work Make questions and then practice them.

a You play tennis.
Do you play tennis?
How often do you play tennis?

b Tony plays tennis.
....

c Jean watches golf.
....
....

d They go to the ball game.
....
....

e She does aerobics.
....
....

f Pete and Dee hang-glide.
....
....

3 a **Pair Work** Student A: You know that your partner plays tennis, goes to the beach, exercises in a gym, goes jogging, gets a health check-up, and stays out late at night. Ask your partner questions using the words *How often*. Student B: Answer your partner's questions.

b **Pair Work** Now change roles.

4 **Pair Work** Role-play an interview.

Student A: You are a reporter. Use the information in the newspaper article on page 98 and interview Gina.

Student B: You are Gina. Use the information in the newspaper article on page 98 and answer the reporter's questions.

LEARNING STRATEGY

Role-playing = pretending to be someone else and using the right language for the situation you are in.

Self-Check

COMMUNICATION CHALLENGE

Pair Work Student A: Look at Challenge 13A on page 125. Student B: Look at Challenge 13B on page 127.

"I like role-playing because it gives me extra speaking practice."

"During class breaks, we talk about things we have done."

1 Write down five new words you learned in this unit.

....

2 Write down three new sentences or questions you learned.

....

....

....

3 Review the language skills you practiced in this unit. Check [√] your answers.

CAN YOU:

Talk about past experiences? ☐ yes ☐ a little ☐ not yet

Find or give an example: ....

Talk about how often things happen? ☐ yes ☐ a little ☐ not yet

Find or give an example: ....

4 What areas need more practice? How can you get more practice? Make a list.

....

....

....

....

5 Vocabulary check. Check [√] the words you know.

Adjectives	Nouns						Question	Verbs
☐ dangerous	☐ accidents	☐ cigarette	☐ indoors	☐ running	☐ swimming	☐ yoga	☐ how often	☐ eat
☐ healthy	☐ aerobics	☐ exercise	☐ meat	☐ skiing	☐ tennis			☐ smoke
☐ racing	☐ alcohol	☐ golf	☐ outdoors	☐ soccer	☐ tobacco			☐ stay up
☐ single	☐ baseball	☐ ice hockey	☐ recreation	☐ survey	☐ volleyball			

14 A Day in the Life

Warm-Up

Unit Goals

In this unit you will:

Make comparisons

"The city is busier than the country."

Ask for and give advice

"I've missed the bus. What should I do?"

"You should take the subway."

Express obligation

"You have to be at school by 9:00."

"Well, I'd like to be a crime reporter."

"I'd like to meet movie stars."

"I'd like to be a political journalist and interview politicians."

1 a Pair Work Look at the pictures above. What is this woman's job? How do you know?

b Group Work Brainstorm. Make a list of all the things a journalist does.

c Group Work Compare your list with another group's list.

2 Group Work Discussion. Imagine you are a reporter. What would you like to do? Who would you like to interview?

3 a Pair Work You want some advice on the following list of topics. Take turns asking questions and answering questions using these models: "Should I . . . ?" "I think you should . . . ."

- visit parents or friends
- go to a movie or a concert
- study or watch TV
- take a bus or a train
- go away for the weekend or stay at home

b Pair Work Think of three more topics you would like advice on. Ask your partner.

Task Chain 1
But the city is more interesting

Task 1

Pair Work Carla is writing an article on differences between city and country living. She interviewed people in the city and the country; here are some things they said. Were these people in the city or the country? Check [√] your answers.

		City	Country
a	It's kind of quiet around here, but we like it.	☐	☐
b	They have to do something about the trash in the streets.	☐	☐
c	There's never anything to do in the evenings.	☐	☐
d	The traffic gets worse and worse every day.	☐	☐
e	The best way to get there is to take the subway.	☐	☐

A I love living in the city. There's so much to do.

B I love the country. It's much quieter.

A The city is more exciting.

B Yes, but there is much less crime in the country.

Task 2

a **Group Work** Discussion. Fill in the chart by writing good and bad things about living in the city and good and bad things about living in the country. Compare your chart with that of another group.

	POSITIVE	NEGATIVE
city life		
country life		

b **Pair Work** Talk about differences between city and country living.

Task 3

Pair Work Draw lines to match the words in column A with their opposites in column B.

Column A	Column B
bigger	faster
noisier	more interesting
cheaper	smaller
duller	quieter
slower	more expensive

Task 4

🎧 Listen. Carla is interviewing Angie and Michael. They are talking about city living versus country living. What are some of the words they use? Look again at the lists in Task 3 and circle the words you hear.

Task 5

🎧 Listen again. What are the positive and negative points Angie and Michael discuss?

	POSITIVE	NEGATIVE
city life		
country life		

Task 6

a Pair Work Skim the following newspaper excerpt and make up a headline for it.

Americans seem to be divided between those who enjoy city life and those who prefer living in the country. Angie Fatakis used to live in the country, but she now lives in the city. "It's so boring in the country," she says. "There are no night-clubs and few theaters." For Fatakis, cities are more entertaining and much livelier.

Mike Boyd disagrees. He thinks that cities are noisier, more expensive, and more dangerous. Says Boyd, "The country is more relaxing—quieter, too. And the people are friendlier and more helpful."

"And more intolerant," adds Fatakis.

"Not so," responds Boyd. "My younger brother has just come out of prison, and he has moved back to the country to live with me. The people here are nicer to him than the city people who knew he'd been in trouble."

b Pair Work Read the article again. Which information is the same as the statements made in the interview in Task 5? Which information is different? What information has she left out? Complete the chart.

c Group Work Compare your chart with another pair's chart.

Task 7

Look back at your chart in Task 2. Can you add to it?

Task 8

You choose: Do **A** or **B**.

A Pair Work Use the chart in Task 2 for ideas. Talk about city life and country life in your country.

B Write your own article about city and country living. Use the chart in Task 2 for ideas.

SAME AS TAPE

DIFFERENT FROM TAPE

MISSING INFORMATION

Language Focus 1 Comparisons with adjectives

1 🎧 **Pair Work** Listen. Then practice this conversation with another student.

A: I really envy you, Carla.
B: Oh, yeah? Why's that?
A: As a journalist, you have such an interesting lifestyle—much more interesting than mine.
B: Sometimes I wish I had a quieter life.
A: Well, I wish my life were more exciting.

2 **Pair Work** Make sentences from these cues and then practice them.

Cues	Sentences
a city / noisy / country	*The city is noisier than the country.*
b rock music / popular / classical music	....
c Los Angeles / big / San Francisco	....
d journalists / interesting / actors	....
e work / boring / leisure	....
f movies / expensive / videos	....

3 Fill in the blanks in the following questions and responses. Compare your answers with those of another student.

A: .....*Is*..... it cold outside?
B: Yes, it .....*is*..... . But it will be .....*colder*..... later.

A: .... you hungry yet?
B: Yes, I .... But I'll be .... later.

A: .... Osaka interesting?
B: Yes, it .... But Tokyo is ....

A: .... Carla busy at the moment?
B: Yes, she .... But she'll be .... after lunch.

A: .... he rich?
B: Yes, he .... But his brother is ....

A: .... we late?
B: Yes, we .... But we'll be .... if we don't hurry.

"Actors are more interesting than journalists."

"Journalists are more important than actors."

"Teachers are the most important."

4 **Group Work** Discussion. How many comparisons can you make between the members of these groups? Use your imagination, and give your own opinions.

a journalists, teachers, actors
b cities, towns, villages
c newspapers, magazines, books
d movies, plays, concerts

Task Chain 2 Dear Deb

Task 1

Group Work Deborah Weissman writes a column called "Dear Deb." People write to her, and she gives them advice about their problems. What kind of advice do you think she gives? What kind of people do you think write to her? Are there advice columns in newspapers in your country?

Task 2

🎧 **Group Work** Listen. Four people are talking about their problems. Listen and identify the problems and the advice.

	PROBLEM	ADVICE
Conversation 1		
Conversation 2		
Conversation 3		
Conversation 4		

Task 3

a Here are some letters from the "Dear Deb" column. Match the letters to Deborah and the advice she gives by filling in the names of the writers in Deb's answers to them on page 106.

Dear Deb

Dear Deb,
I don't have a boyfriend, but I have been out with lots of different guys on a friendly basis. Last month I dated a guy I've known for a year and we had a great time, but he didn't ask me out again. I asked him out once but he didn't seem interested. I even wrote him a letter, but he said he forgot all about it. I know he is interested, because he told my friend Julio that he is. He seems very shy. Am I wasting my time with him, or is he just shy? What should I do?
Scorpio

Dear Deb,
I went out with my last boyfriend for two years, and then six months ago we broke up. I still miss him a lot, but he has a new girlfriend. He called me last week and said that he wants to see me again, but he also wants to stay with his new girlfriend. Do you think I am wasting my time?
Lou

Dear Deb,
My boyfriend and I have been together for six years. We have had some good times and some bad times, but recently my boyfriend started to spend a lot of time with his friends. I told him to choose me or his friends. He chose his friends and made me feel very unloved. Since we split up, he has been coming and going all the time. Now I am very unhappy and don't know what to do. Should I try and get back with him, or should I forget him and make a new life?
Confused

"They could try talking to her."

"They have to make her see that she's making them unhappy."

"They could try giving her more freedom. It might help her grow up."

b **GroupWork** Discussion. Do you agree with the advice?

Task 4

GroupWork Discussion. What advice would you give to this person?

> Dear Deb,
> My husband and I are worried about our daughter. She refuses to do anything we tell her to do and is very rude to us. Also, she has become very friendly with a girl we don't like. We don't trust her anymore, because she is always lying to us. Are we pushing her away from us? We don't know what to do, and we're worried that she is going to get into serious trouble.
> *Worried Parents*

Task 5

PairWork Write your own "Dear Deb" letter. Then exchange your letter with another pair and write an answer.

Dear
Your mistake was to force your boyfriend to choose. His pride would not let him choose you. But he is still hanging around, so he does not want to give you up. Sit down and write out what you really want. When you are sure, sit down with him and talk about what you really want.

Dear
You sound as if you're a very happy, outgoing person. Some shy people are a little frightened of outgoing people. He hasn't responded to you, so perhaps you *are* wasting your time. Stay away for a while and see if he comes after you. If he doesn't, find yourself another boyfriend.

Dear
It will hurt you to hear this, but don't waste another minute with this person. He is not worth it. If possible, take a vacation a long way away from him, and then find yourself another guy—someone who will think of you, not himself.

Language Focus 2 Modals: *have to, should, could*

1 🎧 Pair Work Listen. Then practice this conversation.

A: Tom and Tony have both asked me out. What should I do?
B: Who asked you first?
A: Tony.
B: Then you should go out with Tony, if you've already told him you would.
A: But I like Tom better.
B: Well, you could go out with Tom tomorrow.

2 Complete these statements with *have to, should,* and *could.*

a When you want to make a suggestion, you can use ....
b When you want to give advice, you can use ....
c When you want to express obligation, you can use ....

3 Fill in the blanks with *have to* or *could.* Then compare your answers with those of another student.

a How do I get a license?   You .... take a test.
b Why are you staying home?   I .... study for the exam on Monday.
c How will he recognize us?   We .... wear name tags.
d How will you get there?   We .... take a taxi or the subway.
e When will they study?   They .... study tonight—the exam is tomorrow.

4 Pair Work In each situation, A asks B for advice. Read the conversations and decide what advice A is asking for. Give reasons.

A: What .... ?
B: Well, you don't have to wear a suit, but you do have to wear a jacket and tie.
A: I want to look really dressed up.
B: You could wear a flower in your buttonhole.

A: How .... ?
B: What time do you have to be there?
A: 'Eight o'clock.
B: It's 7:30 now, so you'll have to take a cab.

A: When .... ?
B: What time is the movie?
A: 8:30.
B: You have plenty of time, so you could walk.

Self-Check

COMMUNICATION CHALLENGE

PairWork Student A: Look at Challenge 14A on page 126. Student B: Look at Challenge 14B on page 128.

"My friends and I ask each other for advice in English outside of class."

1 Write down five new words you learned in this unit.

....

2 Write down three new sentences or questions you learned.

....

....

....

3 Review the language skills you practiced in this unit. Check [√] your answers.

CAN YOU:

Make comparisons?   ☐ yes   ☐ a little   ☐ not yet
Find or give an example: ....

Ask for and give advice?   ☐ yes   ☐ a little   ☐ not yet
Find or give an example: ....

Express obligation?   ☐ yes   ☐ a little   ☐ not yet
Find or give an example: ....

4 What areas need more practice? How can you get more practice? Make a list.

....

....

....

....

5 Vocabulary check. Check [√] the words you know.

Adjectives			Adverbs	Nouns				Verbs
☐ bigger	☐ faster	☐ quieter	☐ more	☐ advice	☐ comparison	☐ journalist	☐ reporter	☐ could
☐ cheaper	☐ noisier	☐ slower	☐ most	column	☐ country life	☐ lifestyle		☐ have to
☐ duller	☐ political	☐ smaller	☐ much	☐ city life	☐ headline	☐ obligation		☐ interview

Task 1

Pair Work Match these newspaper headlines to the pictures.

.... **Thunderstorm Hits Atlanta**

.... *Light Plane Crashes in Mountains*

.... **Daring Art Gallery Robbery**

.... FASHION SHOW A HIT

.... *Explosion in Oil Refinery*

Task 2

a 🎧 Listen to the news broadcast and match the news items with the pictures at left.

b 🎧 Now listen again. Where did each of these events happen? Write each of the following places under the correct picture: *Boulder, New York, Cheyenne, San Francisco, Atlanta.*

Task 3

a Read these newspaper reports. Some of the information is different from the information in the radio reports. Can you find the differences? Fill in the chart on page 110.

Picture 1 ....

Picture 2 ....

Picture 3 ....

Picture 4 ....

Picture 5 ....

Denver, Colorado: Rescue workers are searching today for a helicopter. It was stolen by a person pretending to be a flying instructor. The thief ordered the pilot out of the helicopter at knifepoint and took off. Police believe that the thief flew to California.

San Francisco: The Second International Fashion Show is taking place at the Hilton Hotel in San Francisco this afternoon. Designers and models from over 30 countries have gathered for the show, which is one of the biggest in the world.

Austin, Texas: A huge explosion at an oil refinery injured eight workers today. Six of the workers are in the hospital, two of them with severe injuries. The explosion was caused by an oil leak.

New York City: Police are searching for a thief who stole some jewelry from the Blue Chip Diamond Store. The thief got into the store through the air conditioning system. Police say the person was lucky that the system was not turned on at the time.

Rochester, New York: A severe snowstorm caused many road accidents in Rochester yesterday. Police and rescue workers were busy into the night. Authorities expect the weather to improve tomorrow.

	NEWSPAPER	RADIO
Story 1:	Denver	Boulder
Story 2:		
Story 3:		
Story 4:		
Story 5:		

b **Pair Work** Now discuss the differences with another student.

Example: "The newspaper said the aircraft theft was in Denver. The radio said it was in Boulder."

GIMME SHELTER (1970). This is a classic rock-'n'-roll concert movie, featuring the Rolling Stones at the Altamont Speedway in California. This is the best that Mick Jagger has ever sounded. Other groups and singers performing at the concert include Jefferson Airplane and Grace Slick. In the middle of the show, many people start fighting, and before the concert has finished, there is a murder. This movie has great music and great drama. If you haven't seen this movie before, go see it. If you *have* seen it before, it's time to see it again.

Task 4

a Read this film review and underline all the verbs.

b Write the verbs in the correct columns in the chart.

SIMPLE PRESENT	PRESENT PROGRESSIVE	SIMPLE PAST	PRESENT PERFECT

Task 5

a **Pair Work** Listen. Then fill in the blanks and practice this conversation with another student.

A: Have you .... the new movie at the Odeon?
B: Yes, I ....
A: Oh, really? When .... you .... it?
A: Last .... I guess it .... Tuesday.

b **Pair Work** Change roles and practice the conversation again.

Communication Challenges

Challenge 1

Task 1

🎧 **Group Work** Listen and take notes. Then form two groups. Group A: Listen again to Mike and Anna talking about people at a party and fill in columns 1 and 2. Group B: Listen again to Maggie and John talking about people at a party and fill in columns 3 and 4.

	1. YONGSUE	2. PAUL	3. MARIKA	4. PROF. TANAKA
From?				
Description?				
Job?				
Married?				

Task 2

Pair Work Look at the picture on page below. Can you find these people?

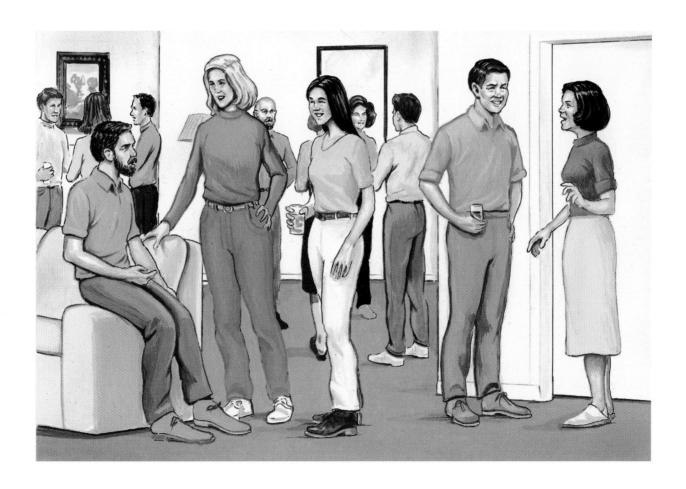

Challenge 2

GroupWork Pick one of these families. Pretend to be one of the people in the photograph. Describe your family. Ask the other students to guess who you are.

Example: "I have a wife and five children. I have two sons and three daughters. I also have six grandchildren. Which person am I?"

Challenge 3A

Task 1

a PairWork Here is a postcard about your partner's photographs. Read it carefully. Use it to answer your partner's questions.

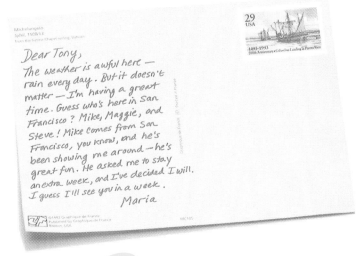

Dear Tony,
The weather is awful here — rain every day. But it doesn't matter — I'm having a great time. Guess who's here in San Francisco? Mike, Maggie, and Steve! Mike comes from San Francisco, you know, and he's been showing me around — he's great fun. He asked me to stay an extra week, and I've decided I will. I guess I'll see you in a week.
Maria

b PairWork Tony is on vacation. These are his photographs. Show them to your partner and ask the following questions:

- Who is in the photograph?
- Where are they?
- Is Tony having a good time without Maria?

Task 2

PairWork Write a reply to this postcard or your partner's.

Challenge 4A

PairWork Read the following comments by singers who impersonate Elvis Presley. Then answer your partner's questions.

George Thomas: I play the young Elvis.
He has a fresh face; he is young and slim. Just like me.

Don Jett: I play the older Elvis. He is at his peak, mature and solid. His voice is good. His personal appearance is good.

El Vez: I play the Mexican Elvis. I like the '50s Elvis. The older Elvis is too fat, so I couldn't play him.

Steve Peri: I play the '70s Elvis. He is a mature man. He is also heavy, just like me. He wears great clothes—flared pants and sequined jackets.

Challenge 12A

A What would you like to do this weekend?

B I'd like to eat out. And I want to hear some live music.

A Well, why don't we go to Lola's Hot Gospel Café and do both things at once?

PairWork You are visiting your partner for the weekend. Think of all the things you would like to do (for example, go out for a meal, go to the movies, go to a concert).

Challenge 3B

Task 1

a **Pair Work** Here is a postcard about your partner's photographs. Read it carefully. Use it to answer your partner's questions.

Dear Maria,
Well, here I am in Florida with my family. The weather is great, but I'm having a terrible time without you. I miss you very much. Everyone else is having fun. My parents are enjoying themselves, and my sister is having a good time. She's going out with a guy she met just after we arrived. Hope you miss me too. See you next week.
Love,
Tony

b **Pair Work** Maria is on vacation. These are her photographs. Show them to your partner and ask the following questions:

- Who is in the photograph?
- Where are they?
- Is Maria having a good time without Tony?

Task 2

Pair Work Write a reply to this postcard or your partner's.

Room to rent in large apartment. Close to stores and transportation. Rooftop deck available. Fully furnished. $420/month. 555-2300.

Double attic room to rent. Perfect for young professional person. $550 per month. 555-3588.

Small apartment to let. Furnished or unfurnished. Close to stores. $500/month. 555-5089.

Furnished room to rent in small house with yard. Transportation available to city. Non-smoker only, please. $300/month. Call Tony at 555-1066.

Unfurnished room to rent. Close to stores and transportation. Good for student or single person. $380/month. Call 555-6429.

Task 1

🎧 **Group Work** Listen. Teresa is talking to a rental agent. Fill in Part A of the rental form.

Rental Agency Information Form

PART A

Name ....

Address ....

Occupation ....

Married / Single

Number of children ....

Type of housing: House / Apartment / Room

Shared / Alone

Price range (per month)

$200–$300	$600–$700
$300–$400	$700–$800
$400–$500	$800–$900
$500–$600	$900–$1,000

PART B

Furnished / Unfurnished

Facilities

• near transportation	yes / no
• near stores	yes / no
• near school	yes / no
• near park	yes / no
• near health club	yes / no
• with garden or yard	yes / no

Task 2

Pair Work Now work with a student from Group B. Decide which of the places at left is best for Teresa.

Challenge 8

Task 1

🎧 Listen to the tour guide. Which places does the tour visit? Check [√] your answers.

	Yes	No
Lincoln Center	☐	☐
Dakota apartment building	☐	☐
New York Historical Society	☐	☐
American Museum of Natural History	☐	☐
Central Park Zoo	☐	☐
Metropolitan Museum of Art	☐	☐
Park Avenue	☐	☐
Bloomingdale's	☐	☐
Plaza Hotel	☐	☐

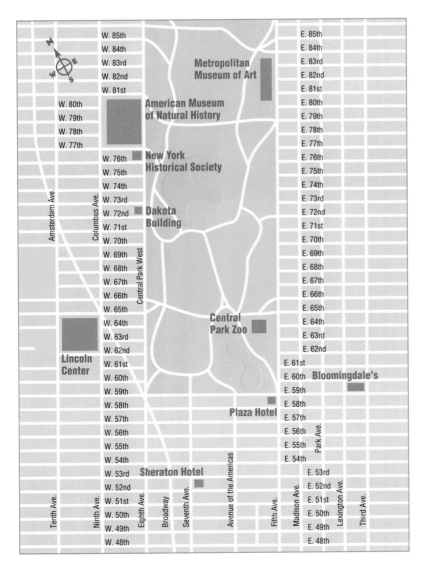

Task 2

🎧 Listen again. Look at the map and trace the route.

Task 3

a **Pair Work** Make up a tour of either your home community or the place where you are studying.

b **Group Work** Describe the tour to another pair.

Task 1

Group Work Read the letter from Teresa to her friend Sandy and fill in Part B of the form.

Rental Agency Information Form

PART A

Name ....
Address ....
Occupation ....
Married / Single
Number of children ....
Type of housing: House / Apartment / Room
Shared / Alone
Price range (per month)

$200–$300	$600–$700
$300–$400	$700–$800
$400–$500	$800–$900
$500–$600	$900–$1,000

PART B

Furnished / Unfurnished

Facilities

• near transportation	yes / no
• near stores	yes / no
• near school	yes / no
• near park	yes / no
• near health club	yes / no
• with garden or yard	yes / no

Dear Sandy,

This is my second week in Chicago, and I'm enjoying it very much. I'm staying with a friend of my brother's at the moment. However, I have to find somewhere of my own, a furnished place I can share. I need to share the house or apartment because housing is so expensive in Chicago, but I like privacy and I need to study, so I really need a room of my own. I'm looking for a place that's close to transportation and stores. It would also be nice to find a place with a yard or a garden.

I hope that I can find something by the time you come to Chicago! I'm really looking forward to seeing you.

Love, Teresa

Task 2

Pair Work Now work with a student from Group A. Decide which of these places is best for Teresa.

Double attic room to rent. Perfect for young professional person. $550 per month. 555-3588.

Furnished room to rent in small house with yard. Transportation available to city. Non-smoker only, please. $300/month. Call Tony at 555-1066.

Room to rent in large apartment. Close to stores and transportation. Rooftop deck available. Fully furnished. $420/month. 555-2300.

Unfurnished room to rent. Close to stores and transportation. Good for student or single person. $380/month. Call 555-6429.

Small apartment to let. Furnished or unfurnished. Close to stores. $500/month. 555-5089.

Task 1

Pair Work How much do you know about the Asian Pacific Rim region? Look at these places. Find the cities and countries and write them in the correct columns.

Ho Chi Minh City	Korea	Tokyo	Australia
Kuala Lumpur	Philippines	Vientiane	Thailand
Republic of Singapore	Indonesia	Seoul	Japan
Hong Kong	Sydney	Taipei	Malaysia
Manila	Vietnam	Djakarta	Laos
Singapore	Taiwan	Bangkok	

Cities	*Countries*
Sydney	Vietnam

Task 2

Pair Work Now draw lines to match the cities and countries and make statements about them.

Example: "Sydney is in Australia."

Task 3

Pair Work You and your partner will each receive a set of clues about the same three mystery cities. Try to name the cities and then compare your clues and your answers with those of your partner. Student A: Look at Challenge 9B on page 122. Student B: Look at Challenge 9C on page 124.

my name is
exercise!
hello
how are you?
where do you live
my sister

Challenge 11A

Task 1

Group Work These were the five most popular and five least popular weekend activities in the United States on Independence Day (Fourth of July) weekend. Work with your partners to number them in order from most to least popular.

.... Going to the theater
.... Going dancing
.... Running errands
.... Going to a sporting event
.... Going fishing
.... Working out, jogging, walking, or biking
.... Working in yard
.... Visiting friends or relatives
.... Reading a book
.... Going to a museum or art gallery

Task 2

Make a list of how people spend time on the weekend in your country.

MOST POPULAR ACTIVITIES	LEAST POPULAR ACTIVITIES

Challenge 7A

Pair Work Ask your partner where the following places are and mark them on your map.

- the library
- the post office
- the bus station
- the school
- the hospital

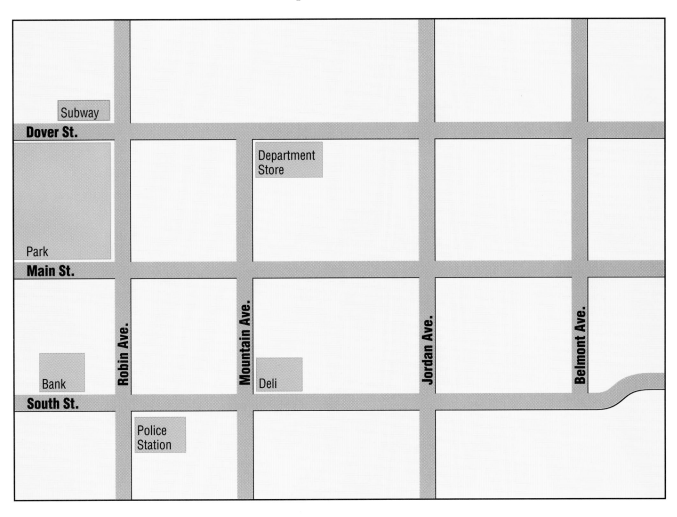

Challenge 11B

Task 1

Group Work Student A has a list of the five most popular and five least popular weekend activities in the United States on the Independence Day weekend. Student C has some information about the activities.

Share the following information to help Students A and C put the activities in order from most popular to least popular.

> Last July 4th weekend, 86% of Americans spent time with friends or relatives. 59% did some form of exercise such as jogging or biking, while only 4% watched sporting events. 5% went fishing. Only 3% of the population went to the theater.

Task 2

Make a list of how people spend time on the weekend in your country.

Challenge 9B

Mystery City 1
- is close to the equator
- is on a small island
- is always hot

Mystery City 2
- has a population of 27.7 million
- is very expensive
- has one of the tallest metal towers in the world

Mystery City 3
- has a population of 3.6 million
- has a famous opera house
- the main language is English, but you will often hear many other languages

Mystery City 1: ....
Mystery City 2: ....
Mystery City 3: ....

Challenge 7B

Pair Work Ask your partner where the following places are and mark them on your map.

- the department store
- the deli
- the police station
- the park
- the bank

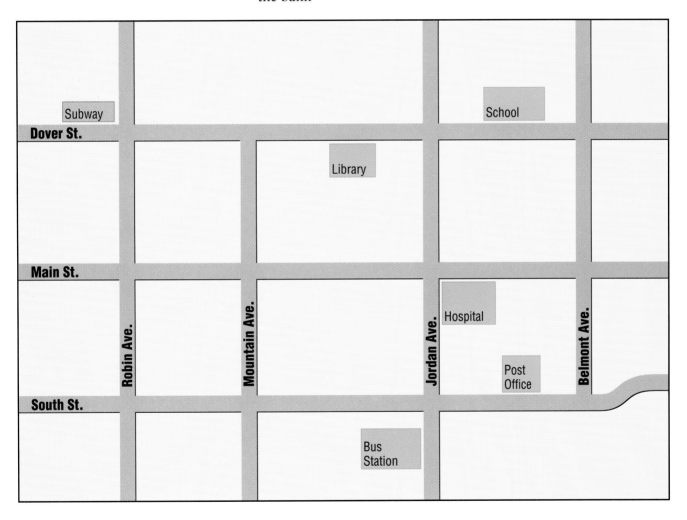

Challenge 11C

Task 1

Group Work Student A has a list of the five most popular and five least popular weekend activities in the United States on the Independence Day weekend. Student B has some information about the activities.

Share the following information to help Students A and B put the activities in order from most popular to least popular.

Last weekend, many people worked around the house: 64% ran errands, while 47% did chores in the yard. 44% relaxed with a book. 7% visited museums and art galleries, and 10% went dancing.

Task 2

Make a list of how people spend time on the weekend in your country.

Challenge 9C

Mystery City 1
- has a population of 3 million
- has four main languages: Chinese, English, Tamil, and Malay
- is a popular tourist destination

Mystery City 2
- is usually hot in summer and often cold in winter
- has a Disney theme park
- was nearly destroyed by an earthquake in 1923

Mystery City 3
- is usually warm in summer and cool in winter
- has a beautiful harbor
- has large immigrant population from over 130 different countries

Mystery City 1: ....
Mystery City 2: ....
Mystery City 3: ....

u're invited... go to the movies! meet me for lunch
what do you do? why
my family neighborhood

Challenge 13 A

Task 1

Pair Work You are going to join a health club. Your partner is a trainer at the health club. Think about why you want to attend the club. Here are some possible reasons:

- to lose weight
- to gain weight
- to get into shape to go skiing
- to get into shape to play tennis

Talk to the health club trainer and answer his or her questions.

Task 2

Pair Work Now discuss what you need to do to get into shape.

Task 3

Pair Work Change roles and do the task again.

Challenge 4 B

Pair Work Your task is to identify the singers. Find out this information from your partner.

a Who plays the Mexican Elvis? ....

b Who is young and slim? ....

c Who plays the '70s Elvis? ....

d Who plays the older Elvis? ....

Now match the descriptions and the photographs and write the artists' names under the photographs.

....

....

....

....

Challenge 14A

Task 1

🎧 Listen. Carla is talking about her job. Take notes about the most interesting, the most boring, and the most dangerous assignments.

Task 2

Pair Work Work with a student from the other group to complete the following. Student A: Fill in the first three blanks. Student B: Fill in the last three blanks.

Student A:
Most interesting: ....
Most boring: ....
Most dangerous: ....

Student B:
Funniest: ....
Most important: ....
Most exciting: ....

Task 3

Now look at the pictures on page 101. Which is the most interesting task, the most boring task, the most dangerous task?

Task 4

Group Work Talk about the most interesting, boring, dangerous, important, and exciting things and the funniest things that have ever happened to you.

Challenge 13B

HEALTH PROFILE

For .... Date ....

1. Weight ....
2. Height ....
3. Pulse rate ....
4. Past illnesses/injuries ....
5. Eating habits (usual foods) ....
6. Smoking habits ....
7. Drinking (alcohol) habits ....
8. Exercise habits ....
9. Reason for joining ....

Task 1

Pair Work You are a trainer at a health club. Your partner has come to you for advice. Ask him or her questions, and fill in the health profile at left.

Task 2

Pair Work Now discuss what your partner needs to do to get into shape.

Example: "You should eat more grains and fruits and vegetables, and you should cycle for 20 minutes every morning. You shouldn't eat so much junk food and you shouldn't smoke."

Task 3

Pair Work Change roles and do the task again.

Challenge 12B

Pair Work Your partner is visiting you for the weekend. Find out what your partner wants to do. Look at this guide and make suggestions.

A What would you like to do this weekend?

B I'd like to eat out. And I want to hear some live music.

A Well, why don't we go to Lola's Hot Gospel Café and do both things at once?

Bijou Movie House
Dracula (R)
5:20 7:30 9:50
The Incredible Hulk (PG)
5:15 7:45 10:15

This weekend at Mitchell Park
The Ice Cream Extravaganza
Featuring over 50 exhibitors and 75 flavors
Admission $12
All proceeds will go to charity

Lola's Hot Gospel Café
The Best Barbecue in the County
Plus: Live gospel music every night
No cover charge!

ANN JONES JAVA JOINT
Music Emporium and Coffee House
This week: Phyllis Jean Beaty and Her Banjo
Live music for all ages.
Cover charge $3

This month at the Science Museum
In the Ames Exhibition Wing
"The Secret Life of Ants"
10 a.m. to 6 p.m. daily

At The Underground Rock Club
Tonight only!
Amy + the Brisbane Babies
Shows at 8:00 and 10:30 p.m.
Call 555-4679

The Aquarium presents
"The Great Barrier Reef"
A special hands-on exhibition and demonstration
Shows at 2 p.m. and 4 p.m. daily

Challenge 14B

Task 1

🎧 Listen. Carla is talking about her job. Take notes about the funniest, the most important, and the most exciting tasks.

Task 2

Pair Work Work with a student from the other group to complete the following. Student A: Fill in the first three blanks. Student B: Fill in the last three blanks.

Student A:
Most interesting: ....
Most boring: ....
Most dangerous: ....

Student B:
Funniest: ....
Most important: ....
Most exciting: ....

Task 3

Now look at the pictures on page 101. Which is the funniest task, the most important task, the most exciting task?

Task 4

Group Work Talk about the most interesting, boring, dangerous, important, and exciting things and the funniest things that have ever happened to you.

Grammar Summaries

Unit 1

1 Pronouns

I	me	my	it	it	its
you	you	your	we	us	our
he	him	his	they	them	their
she	her	her			

2 Statements and yes/no questions with *to be*

I am late.	Am I late?	I'm (I am) not late.
You are early.	Are you early?	You're (you are) not early.
He is from Chile.	Is he from Chile?	He isn't (is not) from Chile.
She is from Boston.	Is she from Boston?	She isn't (is not) from Boston.
It is new.	Is it new?	It isn't (is not) new.
We are right.	Are we right?	We aren't (are not) right.
You are wrong.	Are you wrong?	You aren't (are not) wrong.
They are Japanese.	Are they Japanese?	They aren't (are not) Japanese.

3 *Wh* questions: *what* and *where* + *to be*

What's (what is) your name?	My name's (name is) Mike.
Where are you from?	I'm (I am) from Chicago.
What's (what is) his name?	His name's (name is) Kenji.
Where's (where is) he from?	He's (he is) from Tokyo.
What's (what is) her name?	Her name's (name is) Songporn.
Where's (where is) she from?	She's (she is) from Thailand.
What are your names?	Our names are Sylvia and Maria.
Where are you from?	We're (we are) from Mexico.
What are their names?	Their names are Tomoko and Yumi.
Where are they from?	They're (they are) from Japan.

Unit 2

1 Singular and plural nouns

Regular

		Irregular
boy, boys	aunt, aunts	child, children
girl, girls	uncle, uncles	man, men
husband, husbands	cousin, cousins	woman, women
daughter, daughters	family, families	wife, wives
son, sons		

2   Statements and yes/no questions with *do/does*

Do I sit here?	Yes, you do.	No, you don't.
Do you have a brother?	Yes, I do.	No, I don't.
Does he go to school?	Yes, he does.	No, he doesn't.
Does she have a father?	Yes, she does.	No, she doesn't.
Does it leave soon?	Yes, it does.	No, it doesn't.
Do we wait here?	Yes, we do.	No, we don't.
Do you have sisters?	Yes, I do.	No, I don't.
Do they have cousins?	Yes, they do.	No, they don't.

3   *Wh* questions with *do/does*

What do I need?	You need a work permit.
What do you do?	I'm a teacher.
Where does he work?	He works in a bank.
Where does she live?	She lives in California.
Where do you go to school?	We go to Boston University.
What do they do?	They're students.

Unit 3

1   Present-tense questions with *do/does*: a review

Do I need a student card?	Yes, you do. No, you don't.
What do you do on the weekend?	I study, play tennis, and go to the movies.
Do you like talking about friendships?	Yes, I do. No, I don't.
What does your best friend do?	She's a teacher.
Does she have a close friend?	Yes, she does. No, she doesn't.
Where does he go to school?	He goes to Davis College.
Do we need a ticket?	Yes, you do. No, you don't.
Do they have girlfriends?	Yes, they do. No, they don't.

2   *Wh* questions: *who* + *do/does*

Who do I look like?	You look like my brother.
Who do you study with?	I study with my best friend.
Who does he like?	He likes Maria.
Who does she talk to?	She talks to her friends.
Who do they work with?	They work with Tony and Steve.
Who do you live with?	We live with our parents.

you're invited ... go to the movies! meet me for lunch
what do you do? why
my family neighborhood

Unit 4

1 Simple present with *like*

Do you like classical music?	Yes, I do.	No, I don't.
Does she like rock music?	Yes, she does.	No, she doesn't.
Does he like jazz?	Yes, he does.	No, he doesn't.
Do you like theater?	Yes, we do.	No, we don't.
Do they like modern art?	Yes, they do.	No, they don't.

2 Adjectives

Am I disorganized?	Yes, you are. You're a really disorganized person.
Are you busy?	Of course I am. I'm a really busy person.
Is he good-looking?	Yes, he is. He's a really good-looking guy.
Is she intelligent?	Yes, she's a very intelligent woman.
Is it interesting?	Yes, it is. It's a rather interesting painting.
Are we good?	Yes, you are. You're very good students.
Are they funny?	Yes, they are. They're a very funny group.

Unit 6

1 Modal: *can*

Can I speak to Bill?	Yes, you can.	No, you can't.
Can you call Mary?	Yes, I can.	No, I can't.
Can Tony see the movie?	Yes, he can.	No, he can't.
Can she use your office?	Yes, she can.	No, she can't.
Can we visit you?	Yes, you can.	No, you can't.
Can they miss school today?	Yes, they can.	No, they can't.

2 *How much? How many?*

How many rooms do you need?	I need only one room.
How much is the rent?	Eight hundred dollars a month.
How many rooms does it have?	It has six main rooms.
How much do they pay?	Over a thousand dollars a month.
How many friends does he have?	He has dozens of friends.
How many bedrooms do we need?	We need three.

Unit 7

1 Prepositions: *on, next to, near*

Where is the art gallery?	It's on Miller Street.
Where are the deli and the bank?	They're on Fourth Avenue.
Where is the gym?	It's next to the park.
Where is the hotel?	It's near the subway.

2 Present progressive for actions in progress

Am I studying enough?	Yes, you are studying enough.
Are you working?	No, I'm not working. I'm taking a break.
Is Tony enjoying the party?	No, he isn't enjoying the party much.
Is she watching TV?	Yes, she is. She's watching the news.
Are we working tonight?	Yes, we are. We're working till 9 o'clock.
Are they staying home?	No, they aren't. They're going out.

Unit 8

1 Making suggestions with *Why don't you . . . ?*

Why don't I call a cab?	Why doesn't she visit the museum?
Why don't you go to a movie?	Why don't they go home?
Why doesn't he get a guidebook?	Why don't we go to a restaurant?

2 *There is/there are* and *one, any, some*

Is there a shoe store near here?	Yes, there is. There's one near the subway.
Is there a park around here?	No, there isn't. But there's one a few blocks down there.
Are there any restaurants nearby?	Yes, there are. There are some right by the hotel.
Are there any museums near here?	No, there aren't. But there are some on Fifth Avenue.

Unit 9

1 Adverbs of frequency

Does it always rain in Rio?	Yes, it does. No, it doesn't.
Do you ever go abroad?	Yes, I do. No, I don't.
Does he often come here?	Yes, he does. No, he doesn't.
Does she sometimes take a vacation?	Yes, she does. No, she doesn't.

2   Modal: *should*

When should I go to Thailand?   You shouldn't go in summer or the wet season.
                                    You should go in December.
What should my cousin do in Japan? She shouldn't miss the Imperial Palace.
                                    She should visit Kyoto.
What should we take to Europe?   You shouldn't take much luggage.
                                    You should take lots of money.

Unit 11

1   Simple past: statements and yes/no questions

Did you play golf Saturday?   Yes, I did.
Where did she go last night?   She went to the movies.
Did he go home?   No, he didn't.
How was your weekend?   It was great. I went to the beach and relaxed.
When did they get home?   They got home at midnight.
Where did you leave the car?   We left it in the parking lot.

2   Simple past: connecting words and *wh* questions

I had a great time on Saturday. First, I went shopping and bought myself
some new clothes. Next, I had lunch with my best friend. After that, I
went to a show. Then I danced until midnight. Finally, I went out for a
late-night supper.

Unit 12

1   Present progressive for planned future

What are you doing next New Year's Eve?   I'm going to bed at nine o'clock.
Where are you going on your next vacation?   I'm going to Mexico.
When are you next driving to Maine?   I'm driving to Maine this weekend.
Who are you seeing tomorrow?   I'm seeing José and Carl.
What are you buying next time you go shopping?   I'm buying things for the party.

2   Intensifiers: *too, fairly, pretty, very*

Is that an interesting book?   Yes, it's very interesting.
Is that a good play?   No, it isn't. It's a fairly boring play.
Is the new Tom Cruise movie worth seeing?   Yes, it is. It's pretty entertaining.
Are those TV movies worth seeing?   No, they're not. They're too dull.

Unit 13

1 Present perfect and *Have you ever . . . ?*

Have I ever made you angry?	Yes, you have.	No, you haven't.
Have you ever played golf?	Yes, I have.	No, I haven't.
Has she ever watched a Grand Prix race on TV?	Yes, she has.	No, she hasn't.
Has it ever rained during the match?	Yes, it has.	No, it hasn't.
Have we ever forgotten the tickets?	Yes, you have.	No, you haven't.
Have you ever seen a ball game?	Yes, we have.	No, we haven't.
Have they ever been late?	Yes, they have.	No, they haven't.

2 Time expressions and *How often . . . ?*

How often do you play tennis?	I play tennis about once a week.
How often does she swim?	She swims every day.
How often does he exercise?	He exercises about three times a month.
How often do they play golf?	They play golf about five times a year.

Unit 14

1 Comparisons with adjectives

Are you hungry yet?	Yes, I am. But I'll be hungrier later.
Is Osaka interesting?	Yes, it is. But Kyoto is more interesting.
Is Carla busy at the moment?	Yes, she is. But she'll be even busier after lunch.
Is he rich?	Yes, he is. But his brother is richer.
Are we late?	Yes, we are. But we'll be even later if we don't hurry.

2 Modals: *have to, should, could*

Why are you staying home?	I have to study for the exam on Monday.
When will she be here?	She should be here by eight o'clock.
How will he recognize us?	We have to wear a carnation in our buttonholes.
How do you get there?	We have to take a taxi or the subway.
When will they study?	They'll have to study tonight—the exam is tomorrow.
Where shall we go tonight?	We could try the new movie at the Odeon.
How do I get to the post office?	You could go down First Ave. and turn right. Or you could go left at the subway and turn left again onto Market Street.

Credits

Photographs

Cover Sextant, Courtesy Peabody Essex Museum, Salem, MA. Photo by Mark Sexton; FLORIDA ROADMAP © 1993. Used by permission of the publisher, H. M. Gousha/A Division of Simon & Schuster; © Replogle Globes, Inc. (r); **9** Tracey Wheeler (tr); © Ancil Nance/AllStock (t); © Jun Kishimoto/Photonica (tl); **10** Tracey Wheeler (all); **11** Tracey Wheeler (t); **12** Tracey Wheeler (all); **14** Tracey Wheeler; **15** Tracey Wheeler; **17** © Terry Wild (t); Tracey Wheeler (tl); **22** Tracey Wheeler; **23** Tracey Wheeler; **25** Tracey Wheeler (all); **26** © Kindra Clineff/AllStock (tl); © Robert Holmes/AllStock (bl); © Mark E. Gibson (tr); © Charles Gupton/Tony Stone Images, Inc. (bcr); © Lawrence Migdale/Tony Stone Images, Inc. (br); **27** Tracey Wheeler; **29** © Terry Wild; **31** Tracey Wheeler (all); **33** © Superstock (r); © SCALA/Art Resource (c); © Superstock (l); © Ken Fisher/Tony Stone Images, Inc. (t); Tracey Wheeler (tl); **35** Tracey Wheeler; **36** © Telegraph Colour Library/FPG, Int.; **38** © Bennett-Spooner/Gamma-Liaison; **39** Tracey Wheeler (all); **43** © Chad Ehlers/Tony Stone Images, Inc. (r); © Jane Lewis/Tony Stone Images, Inc. (l); © E. Alan McGee/FPG, Int. (br); © Tony Freeman/PhotoEdit (bl); © S. S. Yamamoto/Photonica (t); Tracey Wheeler (tl); **44** Tracey Wheeler; **45** Tracey Wheeler; **46** Tracey Wheeler (all); **49** Tracey Wheeler (all); **51** © S. S. Yamamoto/Photonica (t); © Richard B. Levine (tl); **54** Tracey Wheeler; **59** Tracey Wheeler (r); © Kazuya Shimizu/Photonica (t); © Yagi/Superstock (tl); **62** © Joseph Pobereskin/Tony Stone Images, Inc.; **64** Tracey Wheeler; **65** Tracey Wheeler; **67** © John Lamb/Tony Stone Images, Inc. (br); © Tony Stone Images, Inc. (bc); © Hugh Sitton/Tony Stone Images, Inc. (r); © Joe Cornish/Tony Stone Images, Inc. (c); © Ed Pritchard/Tony Stone Images, Inc. (bl); © Haroldo Castro/FPG, Int. (l); © Mike McQueen/Tony Stone Images, Inc. (t); **69** Tracey Wheeler; **72** Tracey Wheeler; **73** © Telegraph Colour Library/FPG, Int.; **75** Tracey Wheeler (all); **76** Tracey Wheeler; **77** © Tony Freeman/PhotoEdit (tr); © Tony Freeman/PhotoEdit (l); © Kevin Morris/AllStock (c); © Anthony Neste Photos (r); © Elena Rooraid/PhotoEdit (bl); © David R. Austin/Stock Boston (bc); © David Young-Wolff/ PhotoEdit (br); © Chris Noble/AllStock (t); **79** Tracey Wheeler; **80** © Raymond Gendreau/AllStock (l); © Billy Barnes/PhotoEdit (r); **82** Tracey Wheeler; **83** © Mark Junak/Tony Stone Images, Inc.; **85** © Marc Pokempner/Tony Stone Images, Inc. (tc); © Cathlyn Melloan/Tony Stone Images, Inc. (tr); **85** © Robert E. Daemmrich/Tony Stone Images, Inc. (bl); © Robert Frerck/Tony Stone Images, Inc. (bcl); © David Young-Wolff/Tony Stone Images, Inc. (bcr); © Lawrence Migdale/Tony Stone Images, Inc. (br); © Telegraph Colour Library/FPG, Int. (t); Tracey Wheeler (tl); **86** Tracey Wheeler (bl); Courtesy of Heinle & Heinle (br); Tracey Wheeler (bc); **87** Courtesy of John Steczynski (br); Tracey Wheeler (bl); Tracey Wheeler (bc); **88** Tracey Wheeler; **90** © Al Green/Archive Photos; **91** Tracey Wheeler; **93** Tracey Wheeler (r); Tracey Wheeler (br); © M. Yamazaki/Photonica (t); Tracey Wheeler (tl); **95** © Mary Kate Denny/PhotoEdit; **96** © Eugen Gebhardt/FPG, Int.; **98** © Vic Bider/PhotoEdit; **99** Tracey Wheeler; **101** © William Thompson/Photonica (t); Tracey Wheeler (tl); **106** Tracey Wheeler; **107** Tracey Wheeler; **109** © Scott Dietrich/Tony Stone Images, Inc. (tc); © John Warden/Tony Stone Images, Inc. (c); UPI/Bettmann (bc); © Daniel Simon/Gamma-Liaison (b); UPI/Bettmann (t); **112** © Andy Sacks/Tony Stone Images, Inc. (c); © Frank Siteman/Tony Stone Images, Inc. (tl); © RSI/AllStock (tc); © David Young-Wolff/PhotoEdit (bl); © L. Powers/AllStock (tr); © David Young-Wolff/PhotoEdit (br); **113** Tracey Wheeler (t); **115** Tracey Wheeler (t); **120** © AllStock (tl); © Eugen Gebhardt/FPG, Int. (bl); © Bob Daemmrich/Stock Boston (r); **125** © Schwartz/Gamma-Liaison (bl); © Schwartz/Gamma-Liaison (bc); © Victoria Brynner/Gamma-Liaison (br); © Richard B. Levine (tl).

Illustrations

Mark Kaufman, pages **17, 20, 21, 41, 81**; Bill Thomson, pages **11, 18, 37, 48, 51, 57, 101, 104, 113, 115**

Irregular Verb Chart

SIMPLE FORM ►	PAST FORM ►	PAST PARTICIPLE
arise	arose	arisen
be	was	been
begin	began	begun
bite	bit	bitten
blow	blew	blown
break	broke	broken
bring	brought	brought
build	built	built
buy	bought	bought
catch	caught	caught
choose	chose	chosen
cost	cost	cost
cut	cut	cut
do	did	done
draw	drew	drawn
drink	drank	drunk
drive	drove	driven
eat	ate	eaten
fall	fell	fallen
feed	fed	fed
feel	felt	felt
fight	fought	fought
find	found	found
fly	flew	flown
forget	forgot	forgotten
get	got	gotten
give	gave	given
go	went	gone
grow	grew	grown
have	had	had
hear	heard	heard
hold	held	held
keep	kept	kept
know	knew	known
learn	learned	learned
leave	left	left

SIMPLE FORM ►	PAST FORM ►	PAST PARTICIPLE
let	let	let
light	lit	lit
lose	lost	lost
make	made	made
mean	meant	meant
meet	met	met
pay	paid	paid
put	put	put
read	read	read
ride	rode	ridden
ring	rang	rung
run	ran	run
say	said	said
see	saw	seen
sell	sold	sold
send	sent	sent
shoot	shot	shot
show	showed	shown
shut	shut	shut
sing	sang	sung
sink	sank	sunk
sit	sat	sat
sleep	slept	slept
speak	spoke	spoken
stand	stood	stood
swim	swam	swum
take	took	taken
teach	taught	taught
tell	told	told
think	thought	thought
throw	threw	thrown
understand	understood	understood
wake	woke	woken
wear	wore	worn
win	won	won
write	wrote	written